Voice of the Ancients
Right of Way

By Cha Rnacircle

Ellen!

Enjoy!

Cha March 17, 2012

Science is pushing the date back further and further for the time people populated the Americas... these things could have happened, the people could have existed, did they? What do you think?

Published by:

FriesenPress

Suite 300 – 852 Fort Street
Victoria, BC, Canada V8W 1H8
www.friesenpress.com

Distributed to the trade by The Ingram Book Company

For information on the art work and artifacts see:
chaforthefinest.com
bruceshingledecker.com

Dedicated to the memory of Bruce (Bruso) and Klu (Bernina)

And, a big sign of thankfulness to all my friends and family!

Characters

Yellow Bead Settlement
Godaleda Annee Jimi Dora & Flora Loula Tellero Zeno
Patrel Neosha Meddora Kiisco Booda Thelsie Lynden Oscar
Tug and Uuka

Green Bead Settlement
Eveon Ollieoheh Olivee
Hafpace Quawlee Alocore Vissil Nelva
Wanalee Kip Ira Valita Bernina

Pink Bead Settlement
Paluska Coy Eegeegoo Tahecha Darlone Olgara
Pueda Emma Kelsio

Orange Bead Settlement
Wawaluka and Codesky

Shell Bead Settlement
Zuggerwulte and Guzz

This carving of Eveon and the other characters are by Cha Rnacircle. The artifacts and stone flakings are by ancient people...

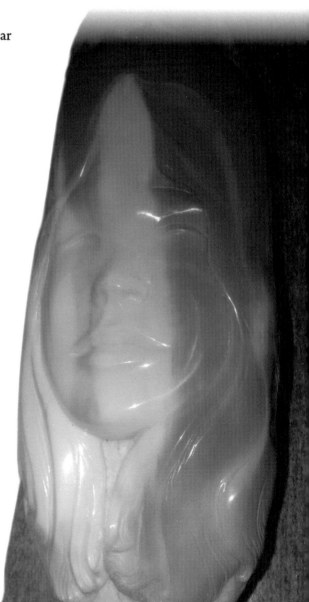

Voice of the Ancients

Right of Way

By Cha Rnacircle

Preface...

When men and women came to this continent forty thousand years ago, an ice sheet covered most of North America. The climate was very different. There was an abundance of food. The animals grew to huge sizes, and so did their predators. I have carved the bones of these animals and have worked with the artifacts of the people. As I held them in my hands, they whispered their stories....Their blood flows in my veins and yours. I am the voice of the ancients, listen.... the story starts twenty thousand years ago in the Midwest...

Chapter One

The animal trails were ancient, hard-packed, deep and wide. The settlement Godaleda and Annee found was on the east side where the trails intersected, north and south. It was built around a hot sulfur spring, which the animals avoided. A more perfect place for living, there could not be... The others who had come before must have thought so too... there were holes cut into the mineral deposits which made perfect pools for bathing by an ancient dwelling. The smooth white walls had been carved from the limestone formation beside it, leaving a platform in the center. Slits were carved into the walls and wood fitted to completely close them. If opened, the tiniest bit of light would reflect around the large room, and illuminate it by striking countless numbers of tiny crystals. The ceiling was of logs which were tightly fitted into the walls like a lid on a box. The heat from the spring kept it warm year round. Godaleda said when they found this place, it had been deserted for many winters.

He said many pottery shards were in the debris around the pools, you could see now that there were scooped out areas near the hot bubbling springs. When a stray drop would land in one, it would sizzle and turn into a yellow powder. The ancient shards had the shape of the scoop.

Annee hung bladders of fresh water into the hot spring. She mixed the yellow powder with fat and ash, she used it to clean wounds. It was slick and frothy when mixed with the hot fresh water. (It smelled better without the yellow powder.) At night the traders would float in the mineral pools and sleep in the sweet grass nearby... putting your bedding out first was important, because your body became so heavy you could hardly get out of the pool.

The traders carried water, food, a kit, their trade goods and a weapon. They traveled light and knew their limits, out running wild animals with a heavy pack wasn't easy.

Shelters were set up along the trading route between settlements, a days journey apart. Many traders would go up two settlements and come back. The route was safer to travel in summer between spring and fall migrations. Some traders from North came in winter, they said it was easier to travel then.

There was a universal language they all understood. They used hand signals and drew pictures in the dirt. Timor came from South, he was more than a trader, he delivered messages. He would come during the full moon, his settlement was far away but he could walk as fast as a bird could fly. The story of their lives hung around their necks. For every winter you survived, you were given a bead of the settlement in which you were living. Timor had many, nine clear stone, seven shiny yellow and four clear purple. In the center there was a flat greyish circular bead with pointy edges, an amulet of some sort. He wore a dark brown leather tunic exposing his long brown arms and legs. His black hair was pulled back into some kind of bun on the back of his neck, and a brown band of leather was tied above his eyes. He had tight fitting flexible sandals. He was brown all over, like the earth...his thick black eyelashes grew straight down to protect his eyes from the dust of the trail. Perfectly balanced, he carried two large quivers and two water bladders with his pack between. He blended into the trail, only his beads sparkled in the sun.

The story beads had another purpose. If a person died on the trail, his beads were taken to the closest settlement. They were hung on the wall of Annees' medical dwelling until claimed by someone from his village.

Godaleda had more beads than anyone.... he had black jet from the south, the dull yellow from the buffalo bone in the plains, sun beads from a settlement on the river, and the blue beads from their settlement. Beads were greatly admired by others, in fact… it formed the basis of the trade route. Godaleda finally found the source of the blue stone, when he became too old for the fast pace of the trade. Their settlement was formed around their children, and the children of traders and hunters whom they had known for many winters. Godaleda and Annee had three beautiful daughters and four sons. Two sons found wives in other settlements and returned with them. One became a trader and went north, one never returned at all.

Godaleda and Annee met at a settlement far away from there where the great bison ate the tall grasses, there were stories of many other animals that hid in the grass and ate them. He was a trader then and she was a young medicine woman. The rule was don't kill anything you can't carry, actually scavenging was easier. The big cats with long fangs would bring down animals and suck their blood, leaving the carcass. Their long teeth prevented them from tearing meat away or even chewing it. If you could get there before the other scavengers you were in luck. Even after they were done feeding, there were still the brains and marrow. Annee healed the wounded and helped the women when birthing. She learned many things, not only how to save a life but when a life should

be ended. She understood the beginning of life, and how to prevent it. When men and women lie together, they do it for comfort, protection and just plain warmth. Juniper berry tea prevented children from coming too soon.

Annees' story necklace began with purple and white shell, the dull yellow next, sun beads, and ended with many blue beads. Godaleda came to her village in time for the great migration, which started before the snow fell. He had heard stories of this place from many traders, it was the farthest settlement northeast.

It was near a deep pool fed from water falling from a cliff. It was built on an embankment over looking a vast plain. Grasslands as far as the eye could see were turning yellow now in the waning sun. The hunters in the settlement could watch the herds assembling for their great migration south. Godaleda was in awe of the numbers of different animals moving together, some he'd never seen. Every day their numbers grew, as they came together it looked like moving shadows of different colors on the horizon. They were being watched by other eyes also, dire wolves, boars, and the many other scavengers of the plains…

The dead animals were easy to spot. The vultures would show the way. The villagers would wait for the nearest kill-site and scavenge. There were many stampedes, being trampled beneath sharp hooves caused the deaths of many hunters and traders, unavoidable when the trading route followed the paths of migration.

On his way up to the settlement, Godaleda was flaking one of his knives in a shelter. A splinter of stone hit his pup's cheek and cut him deeply, it become hot and throbbing and seemed to be getting worse. The pup's big head had caused the death of the best traveling companion a man could ever have. He didn't want to loose him too. He had no other family, they had died in a fire long ago.

Many winters ago, while walking the trading route near the settlement of the Brown Bead, he had come upon a sad scene... A man was lying dead in a shelter with a strange animal at his feet. The animal was not a wolf, fox, or wolverine, but what? By the smell they had been dead for days. As it was getting dark, Godaleda made a fire for protection and began roasting some fresh meat he had taken that morning from a small kill on the trail. As he pondered what to do about the decomposing bodies in the shelter, he heard a sound.... whap...whap... whap... it was coming from the hut! The tail of the unknown animal was whapping the dirt, it was alive!

He got closer and the animals head seemed to lift. Its nose was dry but quivering. Instinctively he reached for his water bladder, poured some into its mouth. It coughed and tried to lift up. Although he was almost overcome by the smell, Godaleda held the animal's head and slowly poured more water into its mouth. He felt the gift of life return to its body and gently eased it out of the shelter.

What was this marvelous animal with fur so soft? As he gently stroked its head, its tail began thumping the ground again. It was the smell of the meat cooking in the fireplace that had its interest... Godaleda cut off a piece and fearlessly put it near the animal's mouth. Amazingly, the creature began to rise up and gently took the meat and chewed it. He filled his own food dish with water. They shared the rest of the meat and the animal soon gathered its strength and went slowly to the stream for a long drink.

Wondering if the animal would return, Godaleda's attention turned to the body. What had happened?? The shelter needed to be cleared for others, the creature had kept the wild animals away but they would soon be back. The stench would *never* leave. This time he would have to go in there with a lighted stick from the fire and see if the man had a story necklace. It was the right thing to do. The decomposing flesh had glued the body to the stone floor. He could see the necklace. He worked it away from his head with a stick. The body was in a sleeping position.

That was as much as he could see in the dim light. When he came out, he threw dry wood into the shelter and with it, some embers from the fire. He then ran down to the stream to breath fresh air and put mud on the story necklace to absorb the smell. He could see the silhouette of the strange animal standing by the burning shelter. He would never forget the deep, sad howling noise it made, the sound went into Godaleda's bones.

The next day he awoke with the animal licking him in the face! What kind of animal was this? The fire in the shelter was gone, only a few wisps of smoke remained... The sun was coming through the trees. Time to move on. As he tied himself into his pack and bladder, he noticed the animal had come back to camp *with the dead man's pack in its mouth*, Godaleda's jaw dropped at such a thing. The animal looked up and its tail went back and forth.

Chapter Two

What kind of hunter would bring an animal to a medicine woman for care? Annee had never seen any living wild animal that closely. She thought it might be a lion cub but it was rounder with shorter legs and ears that hung down so low they meet under its chin. Its head was swollen from the infection. As she spread the healing salve over it, she felt the source...a stone flaking chip. The pup was lucky it hadn't hit his eye...soon snores were coming from the heavy head on her lap, the salve and hot water packs had done their work. With one quick squeeze the whole pussy mess burst apart. The pup kept snoring, feeling no pain at all.

Godaleda was overcome by Annee's gentleness as she touched the wound on the pup with her salve. Water came from his brown eyes, he tried to speak but the words stuck in his throat. She motioned for him to leave, she would let the pup sleep on her lap for a while. It was such a sweet creature and the snoring relaxed her body and soon she was asleep as well. Loula had seen wild animals up close, but never a dog, what a scene it was when she returned from gathering herbs.

Although Annee was a natural healer, she was sharing what she knew and was learning from Loula, a medicine woman with well-known healing ability. A terrible accident left her an orphan. Her mother and father had been taking the old logs from the beaver lodge and floating them down the stream, which poured over the cliff into the pool beside the dwelling. It was a wonderful source of building materials for the villagers. While on top of the lodge, her father slipped on the slick, slimy, pond scum. His leg became wedged among some of the woven branches. The top of the weakened dam broke through, and Quilo was drowned. Trying to return to the settlement, Whela was mauled on the trail by a bear. Hearing the noise, the two men at the top of the falls guiding the logs over started beating the drums and rushed to the commotion. They found what was left of the woman, they grabbed her story necklace and with chests pounding they ran back to the settlement like flying birds. They could hear the bear smashing his way through the brush. It was after them or else coming back to maul the woman again. Oonce took Loula in, accepting her as a gift from the Great Spirit. She taught Loula many things about healing. She took over caring for the community when the ancient medicine woman passed.

The pup, Tug, regained its strength quickly, and was a joy to Annee who treated it like a child....sharing the dogs company with her wasn't exactly a hardship for Godaleda either. He and the pup both stayed in a temporary shelter next to the dwelling where the wood was stored. He had come to this settlement to stay the winter to learn their ways and dialect. He had skills and his strength to offer in return.

Tug was into everything...he loved anything people wore on their feet...At first they thought it was the leather but no, he didn't eat them. He tossed them about, piled them up, rolled on them, slept on them and hid them... Earlier he had learned the real meaning of the word "no" when he decided to eat Loula's herb pouches.... His mouth started foaming, he threw up and surely turned green. He was every bit a playful pup. But... when you said "no" he stopped his antics.

The children loved Tug. His skin was loose and his brown fur was soft and wavy. They would drag him through the dirt and roll him around with whatever he had in his mouth. The children were careful of his cheek, it was healing. Being able to chew now, he ate more, his body was stronger and he began growing!

The location of the village was by a short waterfall, over an embankment. The villagers were able to safely watch the animals gathering, their numbers multiplied as they assembled for the fall migration. The elder said they seemed to be gathering early this season. The huge clouds of dust were gusting towards the south. Never had they seen so many animals, they began in waves of color as they ambled into view. The smaller deer and antelope passed first, smaller and larger striped horses came next. The huge herds of buffalo came later. Sometimes the animals mixed. They were heavy with fat from grazing on the fertile grassland in the northeast. They were moving slowly on their way to the rich southwestern grass lands.

The herds were moving before the tall grasses had turned completely yellow. They seemed to be pushed forward by some invisible spirit....it took a half moon for them all to pass. They would go south until they came to the great river and then turn west. Some would go further south, crossing the river at a wide flat spot.

The villagers had dried and stored enough meat for *two* winters... many tanned hides were stacked in the storage area. They would use them to make garments during the long winter that was coming... Harvesting the grain was next....the hooves of that many animals stirred up the earth and broke apart the dry bones hidden in the tall grass as they passed. The broken bits of bone were also gathered for making tools and beads.

With many hands to work, there was prosperity. No one ever came back to the village empty-handed. Wood was constantly being gathered and stored under a ledge built next to the dwelling. The driest wood would be moved closest to the front entryway. The fires burned endlessly, the winters were dangerously cold.

Stone walls separated the rooms, but a hallway was built beneath the window slots which joined all the doors. Against the outer wall were rooms for wood. It was sorted as it was stacked, wet wood was used for the pit fires outside, dry wood for heat and cooking inside. Wood for torches of different sizes was stacked by the doorway. They would take limbs, smash the tops and dip them in oil. At the end of the hallway there was a place where they relieved themselves. Urine from men was collected in animal bladders for tanning skins, women's urine was tainted. The waste material dropped down on a base of brush and was burned in the fire pits. The disagreeable smell discouraged animal visits. The relief room was also the coldest in the dwelling, or so it seemed, it had no hearth. But, it was better than going outside.

The main opening was at the south, there were eleven rooms altogether. Nine stone rooms were joined in such a way that the hearths met and the heat could be controlled by removing the stones between the rooms. More or less fires could be started, depending on the season. The stone retained the heat and slowly penetrated the structure.

The entrance to the cave of the elders was through the north room. Like the relief room across the hallway, there was no hearth. That is were the hides and grain were stored. The four rooms on both sides of the healing room had four thick, long, wooden shelves. They could be used for storage or sleeping. There was a big space between them and the hearth, which was against the east wall. The structure was roomy and well thought out. The floor was stone covered with hued wooden planks. The center room was for healing. Cooking, story telling and living was done in first room. It was large with *two* window slots and a *huge* hearth. There was a very large entryway on the south corner of the dwelling, which led into a large area they used for working in winter. The hearth in the working room connected to the large cooking hearth. In the coldest of cold, they could cover it and keep the warmth in the cooking area. The entrance to the cave they used as a meat cache was on its east side. Smoke from the hearths would rise up and dissolve into the crevices in the mountain. From a distance it would look like the mountain was on fire.

The structure was snugly fitted into the mountain over the openings of two caves. The ancient builders lived in them while constructing the large dwelling. Old tools, baskets, packs, weapons of all sorts and many other items that had been well made were found stored throughout the larger cave… It was cool and dry but very dark. It was eerie in a way, seeing the belongings of people from long ago. When there was time, elders would look through their possessions. Many useful and intriguing things were found. When people of the settlement passed away, what couldn't be used by others would be stored there.

There were fire holes around the outer ledge of the dwelling for protection, projects, and cremation. They were lit night and day in summer. Drying meat, working skins, and cooking were done over fires closer to the dwelling. Skunks, small wolves, and ravens were some of the small pests who would steal the drying meat. *Then there were the others...The darkness of night enhanced the terrifying sounds they made.*

The view from the cliff was breathtaking… Towards the south was the greenness of the river's edge. Towards the west the yellow grasslands melted into the horizon, the sunsets were dramatic and so very beautiful with every color radiating through the clouds, different every evening. The grasslands blended into the meadows as the land rose to hills then flowed into mountains in the east.

Though you didn't see a bear very often, you knew they were there...the noises they made, felling trees, roaring, screaming and the worst was the crunching sounds they made when they chewed bones.. The deep claw marks on the trees and the huge piles of bear scat when they marked their territory made any man's blood run cold. Some were as big as six men or bigger. They were the most dangerous in the spring when they awoke from their deep sleeps, just plain hungry. They would eat anything and lots of it... Only foolish people would be outside of the settlement at night.

Trails wove throughout the woods behind the mountain. Like the migration route, they were cut deeply into the ground with dense vegetation on both sides. They led to the luscious wild berries in spring and mushrooms in the fall.

The trees were birch, pine, alder, and oak, which cut off a lot of light but protected the berries from too much rain. When they would ripen, the villagers would go into the woods as a group and harvest enough berries for a winter in only three days. The women would pick, the

men would beat their drums and all would sing songs which would keep the animals away, still...

The villagers were a group of sixteen.... The elder was Jimi, his story necklace hung far down with eight purple and white beads and many, many yellow buffalo bone beads from this settlement. Everyone's goal was to be an elder, their lives were so short. Women and children died at childbirth. Hunters and traders fortunate enough to escape the claws of wild animals were forced to leave the trails with serious injuries. One person in thirty lived twenty winters, an elder had forty.

Every spring there was a ceremony of sorts when survivors of the winter received a bead for their story necklaces...The abundance of this settlement was buffalo bones... The older bone would be collected and stored by the wood... Small pieces of crushed bones were the most desirable and easiest to work. The bone was also good for tool making. It made hot, long lasting fires. However, wood smelled better. It was collected after the migration and before the snow...

All the messy, smelly jobs were done outside in summer like drying meat and berries, smoking fish, tanning hides…. Cleaning bladders and intestines for storage, drying sinew, collecting sweet grass for weaving baskets, and flaking flint nodules for tools were some of the other things done outside. After that came the harvesting of wild grain and rice. They began spring preparing for winter. *That is the way people survived.*

Although winters were long, cold and dark, there was much activity inside. The coldest room at the north end of the dwelling was used for the storage of grain and supplies for making the things they needed. Garments, footwear, tools, the only things they didn't make were from the people before them and the wonderful things the traders brought. The settlement had the rhythm of the seasons.

In winter, hides were pulled down and sorted...Although some work was done only by women and only by men, they would take turns doing different crafts...sometimes men would need to sew and sometimes women would need to make hunting tools.

The medicine woman was the exception... things were done for her, but she excelled at sewing and twisting the thinnest sinew from which she also made fishing nets and sewing thread. Most of her time was spent tending to those in need.

Hanging on antler tines that lined the top of the wall beneath the hued wood ceiling, were many groups of story necklaces. Although they were easy to read, the elder would add colorful details in the evenings around the fire. Listening to an elder was the next best thing to being

one. It was a good reason to learn the dialect of the different settlements. The necklaces were hung in groups to represent the many families who had long passed, the empty tines were stories with no ends. Hanging on the opposite wall were necklaces that were brought to the settlement, waiting to be claimed, ending their stories. Listening to the elder was so much more than just stories about the people, he would tell of problems they had. What had worked and what didn't. Although the settlements weren't far apart, they were isolated during the cold winters. Traders and an occasional hunter were always welcomed, bringing news and sharing information. All traders understood a universal sign language, and for more understanding, they drew pictures in the dirt. Most traders were hunters first and they too had a sign language... communication without sound was important when traveling in a world dominated by enormous wild animals. The necklaces of the hunters sometimes had amulets of teeth and claws. To face a bear and tell of it was awesome, to kill one elevated a hunter to a spiritual level.

The last animals of the migrations had passed and as the dust was settling, the villagers were riveted to a horrific scene from the safety of their ledge. One of the giant bears was feasting on the carcass of a buffalo...the enormous size of the creature could be seen without the curtain of grass, which had been trampled down by the passing hooves. The sight sent a chill through the group. Suddenly, from nowhere a short furry creature with a long horn on its snout charged the bear and ran its sharp, curved horn up the length of the bear's thigh. Screaming in agony the bear rose to its full height and crashed his huge paw down on the animal with such force that it broke the creature's back. Screaming and bellowing could be heard for miles while the bear flailed about with a broken animal attached to his leg.

What happened next no one could believe... an animal covered with black hair so long it brushed the ground *appeared*! It seemed to be as large as the bear but stocky and wide with short thick legs. The horn on its snout was as long as half it's body. No one was blinking or breathing as they watched the rhino charge. The force of the impact knocked the bear onto its back...the horn pierced his stomach. The tip burst out of his neck with a fountain of blood... The claws of the bear were locked in a death grip on the sides of the rhino... The noise was deafening. Fur, bones and blood were flying everywhere. The villagers had never seen a rhino before, had it been there all along hidden by the tall grass? Finally, the great bear had a match. It was an animal with the same short temper.

The astonished villagers acted quickly. They dug holes and packed wood to the kill site to build fires to keep other predators away as they began untangling the huge mass of flesh. The second cave behind the dwelling was used as a meat cache... Two of the men began cleaning and constructing more places to hang the meat with wooden poles with tine hooks. The cave was large, they had never filled it before. Their meat of choice was buffalo or small deer, which was easy to pack, easy to store. The skins were the perfect size for their tunics and britches. This would be different...*it could fill the cave.* Leaving the meat to rot in the grass would be wasteful and dangerous. The children were filling water bladders, the men were packing them to the site. They took the drums.

The big rhino was still alive, snorting blood and bellowing. Her agonizing moans filled the darkness of the night as she tried to free herself from the immovable claws of the bear. But where would you strike a death-blow to a creature like that? It was the duty of a hunter to end an animal's life if it were suffering, it was the right thing to do.

The decision was made to stretch the hides on the ground until they dried...they were too heavy and slippery to take up to the settlement. The work took nine men and women five days to finish... The organ meat was eaten on the site...

The bladders were huge, the intestines seemed endless...the vultures waited. Litters were made to transport the meat to the falls...every thing had to be cleaned and salted before it was stored. Fat was cut into small thin pieces for rendering, it was something the children could do. Everyone had a job, everyone was needed.

They all thought of what wonderful things could be made with the skins. It brought much discussion to the group. Getting the hides up to the settlement would be hard... The nights were really getting cold now, soon the ground would freeze and snow would fall. The hides were laying there in the grass. If they froze solid to the ground they couldn't be moved until the next spring. They drew pictures in the dirt of a possible plan to tip them up against the wood storage shelters when they were frozen. They could scrape them from the inside with protection from the wind and cold. It might work... but there were other things to do....

The onions, mushrooms, rice and grain must be harvested. Those who had butchered the beasts needed new garments. Usually, they would make their garments when the snow fell. *What they were wearing now needed to be burned.*

Chapter Three

Days had passed and a chill was in the air as the men went to the site of the carnage to get the hides... their foot coverings stuck to the ground as they walked. The hides were drier and stiffer but still heavy. Flipping them with the fat side down, they would be able to slide the hides along the ground on the frozen layer of dew. The hide was peeled off the rhino legs making them into furry tubes, which were stuffed with grass. While the large hide was still stretched, a strip was started around the outside. One person cut, another person pulled and twisted, and another wound the hairy rope between the stakes now frozen firmly in the ground. The small rhino was larger than any moose they had ever seen...flipping it revealed the reddish-brown silky hair of the youngster. The under-coat was curly and thick. The hair was as long as a woman's leg. They pulled it over the frozen grass and up to the settlement.

Flipping the big hide was much harder, it was heavy, still wet and flexible. The thick black outer hairs were freezing to the ground, what beautiful hair it was, long as a woman was tall. They carefully freed it from the ice, and rolled it onto the skin side. Then, they draped it across their longest pole. They slid and dragged it up. The bear hide was lighter. *Finally their windfall was safely at the settlement.*

One final thing to do...several men went back and freed the heads. They arranged them with the rhinos facing the huge bear. They would drag them to the ant beds in spring. The thoughts of what wonderful trade goods they would make danced through their minds...

Before dawn, the men had dug out a hole in the fire pit. They lined it with alder wood logs and added water. Then, they made a cushion of leaves, and added wild onions and mushrooms. A huge piece of rhino meat was rolled in, and more wild onions spread on top. More logs were added which were topped with stones and firewood. A fire was then lit. It slowly cooked through the day...the sweet aroma was drifting through the air.

The small rhino skin was propped up near the opening of the dwelling's entrance... the women started braiding the long silky hair, they were warmed by the air coming from the dwelling. The large hide was hung over two supporting poles between fire holes. The women were able to braid on both sides. They wanted that hair. It was black and coarse, the undercoat was greasy and filled with stickers and debris, but it was warm and soothing on their cold aching hands. It had a strong but sweet smell, ideas of how to use it drifted through their minds. They tied the thick braids off at the base, cut them and stacked them as they would the wild oats.

The men worked on the bear skin. With the skin side in, they wedged the edges into the rock and stretched it around the north part of the dwelling covering the relief room wall and part of the wood storage area. Using water they froze it into place. Wind coming from north was the worst. It came across the plains with nothing to stop it but the cliff, which was part of the dwelling. The denseness of the skin would hold the wind away from the relief area, which had no hearth.

The fires crackled and sputtered as they dug out the roasted rhino, the rich sweet smell filled the chilly air, the group was tired and ready for a feast.

Finally safe and full, they were all able to relax on the old skins that lined the floor around the huge hearth. Tug was lying on his back dreaming about the delicious rhino toes he had been chewing on all day. Loula and Annee served a tea of birch and rubbed sore aching feet and hands with Loula's healing salve. Godaleda made a place next to him for Annee when she was finished with her chore.

Yes, it was time for the elder to tell them about the story necklaces…

The elder had been a big man, his back bent now with age. His long black hair was streaked with white, deep wrinkles lined his face, his beard was white and thin. His eyes twinkled in the firelight as he put the oil lamp by the wall and started at the beginning. He spoke slowly in the dialect of the village and used the universal hand signs of the traders.

Long ago two men and women came from north where the cold wind starts. They were Rakey and Carrra, Bruso and Kazumee. They had traveled long distances and had been friends for many years. They had come over the endless water to the place where it joined the northwest trade route and worked their way east to this settlement. Then, the people here were living in the cave of the elders. Although the cave was a wondrous place and a home for many, Rakey and Bruso said connecting the two caves would make it safer going to the cache for stored meat and water, and they could have a safe place for relief. Everyone agreed and all that winter they planned the dwelling. It took three summers to complete.

Rakey and Carrra were both tall with light colored skin and hair. Her hair was long and thick, the color of dark straw. She brought ideas from north, too. She had a curved knife and used it with great skill to filet fish and jerk meat, it also cut skins. She shared many stories about the Great Spirit and customs of the north. The story necklaces were one. Hers had beads that shined like the sun as did Rakeys', some were black. The first buffalo beads were made for her necklace.

Then, the elder held up the oil lamp and illuminated the corner. A huge well-worn adze stuck deeply into the wall where Rakey left it when he finished his work on the dwelling. Notched into the wood beside it was a knife with a curved blade, both had the sign of water carved into the handles.

Beneath the adz and oolu were the story necklaces of Bruso and Kazumee, they were entwined. They both had black and shiny sun beads. There were four buffalo bone beads on Brusos' and many buffalo beads on Kazumees'.

Bruso was a big man with thick black hair on his head and face. His body was soft, not like rugged Rakey. Kazumee, his wife was so very tiny she looked like a child. She had slits for eyes, her nose was short, her skin yellowish and hair so black, it was blue in the sun. She too used the curved knife.

Bruso and Kazumee brought much joy and laughter to the village. He drew pictures in the dirt and made designs for people to carve into their tools and weapons to show ownership like Rakeys'. Sometimes he put pictures on the hides. Kazumee told stories of her origins, a place farther away than Carrra and Rakey. She shared her knowledge with the children and cared for them in the day when the women did their work, she was much loved. The group wondered how she could have come so far on such short legs.

The villagers had moved into the new dwelling before the third winter, there was much happiness. There was also much snow and it was very cold. Suddenly it became very warm and the snow melted, then it became very cold yet again. The snow turned to ice and it snowed even more. Bruso had gone for water with no tether and became lost in the whiteness...he was found frozen with a load of icicles in his arms.

That spring with much sadness in their hearts from the loss of their dear friend, Rakey and Carra left the settlement to return to their people in the far north where the cold wind began...

There was a big sigh from the group when the elder finished speaking. He blew out the oil lamp. The story had many lessons, it made them grateful for what they had and gave them much respect for those who came before.

Those who could, got up and went to their rooms, the others slept right there. Tug was lying on a big pile of foot coverings snoring and whimpering. Godaleda gently picked the pup up and went to the men's sleeping room. They passed the medicine room where Annee and Loula stayed. Many thoughts passed his mind about Annee, many thoughts. Had he ever looked into blue eyes before? Just passing the healing room made his chest thump.

Chapter Four

Loula loved teaching Annee about healing. Many times Annee with her nimble fingers assisted her mending wounds. Using the coarse rhino hair was in her thoughts now. They took a braid to the healing room and looked at it... First they soaked the hair in salt water. Loula showed Annee the tiny bugs that floated up. Then, they dropped the whole braid into bubbling, soapy water by the hearth. The black color was easy to see against the skin. Two tools were used to sew a wound, a small wedge shaped stone flake bound to a handle, and a tiny bone hook. A cut was made, a loop of sinew was caught with a hook and pulled through. Sometimes Annee just held the oil lamp so Loula could see. Loula would pierce the skin with the blade but the sinew was skin colored and wasn't even. It was hard to pull through. The rhino hair was better. They would both practice by stitching little pieces of tanned hides together. Annee practiced so much, she started doing sleeping covers. It was a way to use the extra tanned scraps.

There were many foot problems...blisters, sores between the toes. Toenails growing too long would weaken the foot coverings letting in dirt. It would cause irritation, then infections, and death. Rawhide soles were strong and durable but would get mushy when wet and the bad smell would cause infections.

When badly wounded, Loula would give the injured person a choice, a drink of hemlock or birch. If they took the birch, she would do the best she could. If he chose hemlock, she would try new methods…. Infection and loss of blood took most of them.

A hunter came to the settlement one winter for hemlock. He'd fallen through the ice by the beaver lodge, the bottom of his feet were black. He gave Annee his story necklace and offered all his possessions to Loula to end his life. She gave him the poison cup. As his spirit was leaving his body, he told a story. He saw vapor coming from a shelter thinking it was another hunter, he crawled in, but, it was the den of a sleeping bear. It wouldn't awaken to take his life. He said he slept with the bear but the heat from its body brought agony back to his legs. He clutched the hands of Loula and Annee in thankfulness as his spirit left his body. His pain was ended.

They took his story necklace and put it on the wall. He had a few green beads from the settlement below but many pink and black beads. When they were sure his spirit had left the healing area they returned. They decided to look *in* his body. His tunic was heavy and wet, thawing there in the warm healing room. They peeled it away, revealing an older man. His body was bright red and swollen. His feet, legs and hands were black. Their eyes hurt to look at him. He had many scars. One long one across his middle region was red. Loula wondered how he might have recovered from an injury so big. The edges of the wound looked ragged. They could see big round scars left from sewing it together. Curiosity came over her. Annee held the oil lamp closer as Loula made a long cut above the scar and pull back the skin...they both ducked in case the spirit was still *in* there...

They looked in amazement, his intestine had been cut, sewed back and he lived! Could that be? There were lines of white tissue going around and around squeezing the intestine almost closed. No wonder he wanted hemlock. Another thought came to her. She moved Annee's hand holding the lamp closer as she lifted the ribcage and looked in. She put her hand on the still warm heart, it was plump and red, they saw many connections. She told Annee this was where the throbbing came from… The

spirit
lived in
there and
pushed blood
through the body…
Sometimes the spirit
got tired and slipped away.
You could feel and hear its
strength. She held Annee's
hand to her neck and then
wrist. Annee felt her own neck,
the throbbing was very strong.

The thought of sewing a wound inside the body sat in Loula's mind. The rhino hair hung over the hearth. They wondered who would need it first…

You could see the change in Tug every day. He would go from room to room looking for foot coverings, which he took to the front entrance. The cooking area was a favorite spot of his. It was the day after the rhino feast and the smell still lingered. He helped Thelsie keep the floor clean.

She tied him to the outside tether and let him go for relief. As she was coming back into the dwelling the sky got dark, and a huge bird swooped down and flew off with the pup. His

talons
were
locked in
Tug's loose
skin. The bird flew,
well, until the tether
had no more slack…
The pup's head jerked
down and they both came
crashing to the ground. Jimi
and Godaleda pried the talons out
of the pup's back and he was once again in the healing room.

Loula and Annee cut the hair off around Tug's wounds, applied the healing salve and used the rhino hair for the first time. Annee held the lamp for Loula and watched her stitch Xs over two of the tears. Loula held the lamp for Annee as she did the same. Tug didn't flinch, he was in a deep, deep, sleep. Loula pulled back the loose skin around the pup's mouth and looked at his teeth. Huge molars were exploding from his gums. She rubbed them with the healing salve, he tried to moan but just let out a breath... They wondered if he was going to grow into a bear.

The rhino hair was good for sewing wounds. She had tried her own thick hair, but the knots wouldn't hold. There was something else she wanted to try....

For many years Tellaro and Oscaro had hunted buffalo together.

There was one *magnificent* creature, bigger than all the rest. They loved seeing him. They could feel his spirit when he passed. They had seen him fight and kill a bear but not before the bear's claws sliced his nose. He lived on... They saw him many times guiding the herd. Towards the end of summer they came upon him. He was lying in the grass, barely alive after being mauled by a giant cat with long teeth. They couldn't leave him there to die slowly or to be eaten alive by wolves. Oscaro told Tellaro he had to give him the death blow. As Tellaro touched the animal's neck, it jerked around, probably thinking the giant cat had come back. One of his horns caught Tellaro's eye and pulled it completely out of the socket. Though his eye healed with no infection, part of Tellaro's spirit left him.

Tellaro had been full of energy and fun, a delight to be around. He was also good to look at, thick glossy black hair, which he tossed around, dark twinkling eyes... He could carry a deer on each shoulder, he had flaked the tiny blades Loula used in her work. He had brought her the valuable pouch of bear bile from the carnage. He made many women's chests pound, including hers. She had lain with him from time to time. When he wanted her, he would call "Lulu" and they would sneak off to the storage room where the tanned skins were stacked. Thinking of those times always brought a smile to Loula's face.

Since the accident Tellaro stayed by himself and did only what was needed, he avoided everyone's gaze. That night he did come to her. He brought his story necklace and asked for the poison cup of hemlock, he said he was just half a man with no eye. He would never be able to hunt again and wanted to release his spirit. With mixed feelings she said if it was his wish, but it was her wish to try something. She whispered it to him. He thought about it, agreed, and drank the birch. As he lay on her table, she cleaned his face and braided his long, glossy hair back. He became sleepy. She had Annee hold the oil lamp. With her tiniest stitches, she sewed his eyelids together over the empty socket with the Rhino hair...

Thelsie and Booda lived with their daughter, Lynden, in the room by the cooking area. They took on the duty of cooking for the group, and through the years they had gotten better and better. They had come from the settlement of the Green Bead by the river and had made many things with the sticky clay there. They had learned to make clay vessels for trade, it was summer work. They came to this settlement for the fall migration, and stayed. Many hands were needed for processing the animals. Thelsie made her own cooking vessels which they had brought up to the settlement on a sledge over the snow early one winter. Everyone loved her vessels, they all had holes for hanging over the fire. Several had lips which made it easier to pour water and rendered oil into the bladders and into the intestines for storage. Some of the pots were very large. *This year they had rhino and bear fat…* There was so much, they started just stacking it in the back of the meat cache.

The men were in the cooking room boiling the bear paws. *They* wanted the claws, *Tug* wanted the bones. When the claws were ready to release, they fished them out and threw rhino toenails and deer hooves into the thickening water. Once before, they had made glue in one of Thelsie's pots. It cooked too long. When it cooled the glue wouldn't come out. She hung it in their room by one hole so they wouldn't forget what they'd done. The next summer, the men made a special trip to the settlement of the Green Bead to get more pots for Thelsie and some for themselves.

The claws were longer than a woman's hand, the bones came out easily. They would be good for trading. If a hunter had killed a bear, the claws and long teeth would be his to wear, but since these were a gift from the Great Spirit, they could trade for things for the dwelling. They talked as they worked. Salt was needed for jerking meat and special herbs from far away were needed by Loula.

Gathering everything for making the foot coverings was nearly done. All of them had wood formed in the shape of their own feet. A thick, wet piece of hide would be laced with sinew and then stretched over the form. When dry, they would use the same holes to attach the softer leather tops.

After the women had finished braiding the long hairs of the *big* rhino, the men flipped it over to the raw side…the next day they scraped, and scraped and scraped… Finally, they were able to cut the sides into strips. The rhino hide was **so big**, one leather side strip would be enough for *all* of them. They still had to get the rest of the frozen hide through the front entry-way, through their work area, and into the cave opening of the meat cache. It was now shaped like a frozen furry tunnel and so big a man could walk under it. Three more cuts and they were able to get it through. Finely, their bounty was safely propped up against the far wall of the meat cache.

Tellaro could feel the hot bloody breath of the buffalo on his face and the pain of its horn in his eye, he could feel the buffalo's tongue on his cheek and woke with a start.......

Tug......

He picked up the pup and felt his way down the hallway to the outside entrance for relief. Both Tellaro's eyes were swollen now and he picked up some of the light snow and held it to his face. This was the first time he had ever felt bad after being with Loula. He held some snow on Tug's hairless back over the swollen black Xs. Tug pulled away and ran to the large feathered bulge under the snow. He grabbed a wing and started pulling. Tellaro cut the huge wing away from the bird, tied it to the tether and began throwing it out and pulling it back. Tug watched, then ran and pounced on it. Tellaro drug them both back and threw it out again. A game! Soon Tellaro untied the wing from the tether and threw it out. Tug brought it to him, they did it over and over.

. A tap came to Tellero's shoulder. There was a hand with a steaming cup of tea. He laughed, his first laugh in many moons….

There were two children in the settlement, Dora and Flora, sisters of Annee and daughters of the elder, Jimi. They were born at the same time, matching, they looked exactly alike. Jimi said it happened because his wife was terribly frightened by a huge hairy creature with a long nose when she was carrying them. He felt sorry and ashamed now because he didn't believe her, her story necklace was on the wall.

The children were the first to have their foot coverings made, two matching pair. Their feet were growing but they only needed two foot forms. Their feet were measured and the hide cut.

They picked out the burrs and debris themselves before they dropped them into the pot to soak. Next were Loula and Annee, their foot forms already made. Then Thelsie, her daughter Lynden and husband Booda. Medora and Kiisco had the room between the men's sleeping rooms and the healing room. They had wanted children, but they would come too soon with no spirit, it was very sad. She and Kiisco took care of the children, he Jimi was very grateful.

Next were the big feet. Jimi the elder was the size of a man and a half, with huge hands too, he was still very strong. He carried wood for the fires and made sure they burned continuously. He only left the settlement for wood. It was safer and easier to get in winter. In the spring he would listen for the bears pushing down dead trees in the forest when they looked for grubs. As things started to freeze he would go to the downed trees and free them up. When the snow was right they could be easily moved.

Next were Tellaro and his good friend and hunting companion, Oscaro. Tellaro seemed to have forgotten about his missing eye with all the excitement of new foot coverings. Oscaro and Tellaro met at the settlement of the Green Bead. They preferred hunting to trading and brought many hides and good meat to the settlement. They both wore the teeth of a large bear, which they had killed together.

Neosha and Petrel lived to trade. They could hunt and cook, but they were usually thinking of things other people in other settlements might want. Their foot coverings were important. They seemed to use more than the other men. They would always be in the healing room getting their toenails cut, and getting healing salve for their sore feet from long trips. They had many stories about what they had seen and what other settlements were doing. Neosha and Patrel gathered the new ideas and shared them with the group.

Zeno was staying the winter in the Yellow Bead Settlement to learn the ways and dialect. He had come from far west by the endless water. His story necklace had seventeen purple shell beads. He did some hunting and trading but enjoyed making things from wood, especially alder, which was new to him. He had more than seventeen winters, but hadn't stayed a whole winter anyplace to earn more. He liked animals, and didn't want to kill them, he really wanted to *ride* them! He had made everyone spoons with holes. He had also made Tug a big bowl with the sign of water around the top. Tug had been eating and drinking from everyone's food dishes. Zeno had a curved stone adz. It was hard to flake but worth the effort.

Chapter Five

Remembering the large eagle talons, Tellaro went back outside to the huge dead bird with Tug at his heels. With two quick snaps, he broke the legs off. He pulled out the tail feathers and ripped off the other wing. The wings were tipped with green and yellow, pretty… Tug was ready to play but Tellaro went to the pond for some ice for his face. Water was still flowing down the cliff, but the edges of the pond were freezing up. A path led to a ledge behind the falls. Although the water was cold, it was a place the group could bath and wash their hair. The entrance to another cave was there too. The drop off behind the ledge was deep, and it was always flooded. They wanted to go in but *it was hard to get a lit torch under the falls.* During the warm days in summer, he, Patrel, Neosha, and Oscaro would sit on the ledge in the spray, chew peppermint leaves and dangle their feet in the cool, foamy pond water. They had dug a small pool beside the large one, which they could use for bathing, cleaning things and tanning hides…

it could be heated with hot rocks from the outside fires. He turned and looked out at the vast grass plain, which was covered with a light dusting of snow glistening in the afternoon sun. It made everything look so clean and fresh. He could see the outline of the bear and two rhino heads against the horizon.

He was thankful he hadn't drunk the hemlock.

A funny sound was coming from Tug. He was standing stiff looking at the woods. Tellaro grabbed the pup up and quickly ran to the safety of the dwelling.

Medora was the last one to come to the cooking room that morning. Thelsie was making flat bread with the fresh grain and acorns the men had ground for her the night before. Peppermint tea was on the table. Bowls of raw rhino hide were soaking by the doorway to the entry room. At the outside hearth, an occasional hoof bobbed to the surface in the pot of glue. Medora fell to her knees and threw up. They all knew what was wrong… It wasn't the combination of smells either.

Zeno wanted to work in sunlight. The door had to be closed now and the window slits were tightly fitted with wood closing out the cold, animals, and *light*. The wood plugs had to be put in from the outside and locked in place from the inside. He was thinking about a frame like a drum with a gut covering.

Godaleda was in a corner winding a rhino hair around an arrow shaft wedging an arrowhead into place, a little bit of glue would hold it tight. The arrow would have a smooth and deep entry. Tellaro was watching intently, he liked the shape of Godaleda's arrowheads. He gave him some of the green and yellow tipped feathers from the big bird that took Tug for the end of the arrow shaft. It was the biggest eagle anyone had ever seen, it should make their arrows fly high. Tellaro thought of hunting with just one eye, could he even *aim* his arrow? Tellaro was also trying to think of trail signs to ask him about Tug. Tug was lying on their feet crushing the soft bear bones with his budding molars. His stitches were looser, his wounds were healing rapidly.

The twins were sitting back to back braiding rhino hairs in strands of four. They folded two to start, which made a hole for the hook. Everyone wanted braided rhino hair for their foot covering. Their tiny fingers and good eyes, perfect for the job. Neosha was wondering how many they could do in a day, the braids might be good for trading.

Kiisco and Patrel helped Booda get a rack of buffalo ribs from the cache and tie it up around poles in the hearth, they then went back to the site of the carnage for their rope.

Jimi wanted to gather wood, Zeno wanted to find the right branch for his frame. Thelsie and Lynden wanted mushrooms. Medora wanted fresh air. They grabbed baskets, a drum and went to the woods.

The forest floor was frozen and quiet. The light snow hadn't gotten past the dense tree tops. The forest smells were so refreshing. Yellow, cupped mushrooms had popped up through the rotting leaves before they froze. They were everywhere and the kind they wanted. The women quickly plucked them up and laid them in the baskets, there were so many they would have filled the whole meat cache.

Zeno found some limbs for his thought and was helping Jimi free his two fallen trees. **Then,** they could hear the labored breath of a bear coming up the trail, it had a hump on its back. It was smaller than the huge bears but faster too, and unpredictable. You could see the fat jiggle on his body when he took a step. Jimi whistled a signal of danger to the women. Everyone stood perfectly still as the huge grizzly lumbered up the trail towards them. He stopped right by the women, raked up a paw full of mushrooms, ate them and went on his way. Still, no one moved until he was out of sight down the path.

Ever so quietly, the group with chests pounding, picked up their bounty and moved quickly to safety. They pulled open the heavy door. The heat and smells of the dwelling brought Medora to her knees throwing up yet again. Jimi told the others that she will have matching children now.

Patrel and Kiisco made their way down to the site for the raw hide strips they had twisted. They pulled the stakes from the ground leaving a very long skein of frozen rope. They put one end on each shoulder, it was cold but easy to carry. They went over to admire the animal heads, now frozen solid, dusted with a layer of snow. The red sun was sinking in the west turning the heads a pinkish-orange. As they started back to the settlement, they could see some of the group on the ledge looking at the glorious sunset, too. They could hear their excitement as they got closer, *they could also hear the drums.* They walked faster, not really wanting to turn around. Others in the group ran down the trail, took their load, and forced them up to the safety of the ledge. They took a breath and turned. Silhouetted against the horizon behind the heads, were five huge beasts moving slowly across the plains. Were they more rhinos? They seemed bigger. The group watched as long as the light permitted. The aroma of baking buffalo filled the cold air.

Again they were all gathered around the great hearth in the eating room. Booda had put a pot of water under the buffalo ribs to catch the drippings. He was already making soup for the next day. As they finished eating, they threw the bones into the water with fresh mushrooms and onions. They had done a lot that day. Half of the soles of the foot coverings were stretched and drying on the forms, the braided rhino cord was ready. All of Godaleda and Tellaros' arrows were tipped with freshly flaked stone, wound with rhino hair and had green and yellow tipped eagle feathers slotted into the ends of the shafts. Zeno had peeled the bark from his wood and began forming the shape of the window slot, he needed wet wood and steam to bend it, his undertaking smelled good. The women had strung the mushrooms like beads on sinew cord. Mushroom necklaces were criss-crossed back and forth across the top of the room to dry. Tug was lying on his back in the pile of foot coverings, a good sign that his wounds were healing.

The fire was crackling, it was time for Jimi to tell more stories.

Jimi took the oil lamp and told the group that HE wanted to hear a story. He wanted to hear about Godaledas' settlement and how he came to have Tug. They all agreed and sat up to listen. Godaleda was surprised and his chest started thumping as Jimi put the oil lamp in his hand. Taking a deep breath, he started very slowly using signs and some of the dialect he had learned from the group. "He" (he put his hands on his chest) "came from south," (he blew a long breath and arched his arms again to his sides) "he had 16 winters" (he held up both his hands, clinched them and held up one hand and thumb). "His settlement" (he pointed to the walls) "was hot" (he panted and made the sign for hills) "had many" (he opened and closed his hands many times) and pointed to the walls. "But"

He wanted to say it burned. He went to the hearth and took a piece of wood and swept it around the walls. They were all happy with his explanation and pulled Tug off the pile of foot coverings and pushed him over to Godaleda.

Godaleda was smiling and trying to find more signs and words. He made the sign of walking (steps) (hills) the sign of a shelter (two hands together like a dome) the sign for death (two fingers on each eye) person (he laid on the floor the way he had seen the man in the shelter) he held his nose closed to try to show a bad smell. He rolled Tug into the position of the animal next to the dead man (himself) and put the two fingers of death on each eye. They were both lying on the ground.

The group had all gathered around to watch and listen. He made the sign of Mother (cradled arms) and pointed to Tug. They seemed to understand. He put his fingers back over Tug's eyes and pulled them away quickly and put the sleepy pup on is feet. He made the sign of two winters (holding his hands like a disk in the air and moving it from side to side twice). He made the sign of love (crossing his arms over his chest) and petted Tug. He made the sign of a companion (one arm over his chest and one arm in the air over someone's shoulders). Tears came to their eyes.

How could he explain the next part? He pointed to the sleepy pup's stomach and then pretended that Tug was giving birth. He pointed to Tug's big head and then put the two fingers of death on Tugs eyes. Some of the group was weeping, that was a sad story. Loula asked what animal? She made the sign of bear (she mashed her nose and made her ears cup) or wolf (puller her nose long and her ears up) or lion (two fingers in her mouth for long teeth). Godaleda shrugged, he pulled his nose and his ears up for "Wolf" and two fingers in his mouth for lion and shrugged again. He pointed to Tug and made the sign of "Mother" again trying to show a bigger animal that came to his

thigh. Tug was on his back again after the demonstration. They all loved Tug no matter what kind of animal he was.

Godaleda gave the oil lamp back to Jimi. Jimi told the group that some one should watch the animals they had seen on the horizon. They could be a danger to the settlement. The bears would soon be sleeping in their dens, they were the worst. There were three kinds, giant bears, the grizzlies and the short faced bear. Jimi hoped they would all be as fat as the one they had just seen and would sleep hard.

Jimi watched after the group, gave them advice and helped with their plans. He was the oldest person in the settlement and the largest. Work was easy for him. He tried to make it easy for the others. He could carry the weight of two women. He could fill and lift the heavy water bladders up to the tine hooks above the hearth where they would warm up. He would take water to the relief room so the group could bath, sometimes he would take hot rocks from the hearths in to **warm** the room. Having the bear skin outside, covering the relief area made it **much warmer.** He would also remove the *relievings*, which were freezing now. The relievings would drop down on dead brush through a hole in the floor. Jimi could pull them out through the wood storage area. He would burn them in the fire holes farthest away. He stored the bladders the men had filled in the wood storage area to be used for tanning the next year. He had done that for eight winters, all the time he had been there. Going out side for relief was uncomfortable and very dangerous. It had an outside entrance by the first room of wood. Having the protected relief room and the connecting hearths made their lives longer and it made them able to be more productive in winter. They had time to make things for the trade route, they didn't just have to worry about surviving, they could enjoy living.

This was the best settlement Jimi had ever been a part of. He was from north. His family had to leave their dwelling because the cold ice was coming closer and closer and would soon cover it. They went east to another settlement where he met his wife, Althea. They had two children there but a strange sickness came and took his son's spirit and many of the others so he, his wife, and Annee came west to this settlement. He had ideas for growing plants and brought seeds with him. He had grown grain in the northern settlement, he needed the right place. Here, grain was already growing, it was the *perfect* place. Wild rice and cress grew in the marshy area by the stream.

The deep pool beneath the falls fed a stream that eventually went into the river by the settlement of the Green Bead. It followed the cliff.

Between the stream and the drop off for the migration route was a flattened area. The walls of the settlement were built with stone from that area leaving the good soil. Jimi's seeds grew well there. They harvested the grain and ground it for bread. The area was protected from the trampling hooves of the migration however, not from the other creatures. Two winters before, his wife Althea, and Annee went to harvest and startled a long toothed cat sucking the blood from a deer who had been feeding on the grain. Annee escaped the cat's sharp claws but Althea did not.

Jimi felt the long skein of rope the men had brought and laid in the hallway. It was thawing now and would soon be flexible. It was long enough to reach up and down the hallway four times.

That morning Madora avoided the entry room. She, Annee and Loula wanted to start the new tunics they all needed. They decided to work in the healing room. It was large, very clean and had two big tables. Jimi suspended two large oil lamps from the ceiling for them. They measured him first, he was the largest. They picked out the largest buckskins, put them together smooth sides in, tail ends up. With his huge arms out, they marked a spot under his armpits and down the sides with a charcoal stick.

They trimmed off the extra buckskin and began to sew, four lines of stitching was all it took. Working together they could do six tunics in a day. They made them to be worn on both sides. Winter tunics would have hoods of leather or fur for warmth. Godaleda and Zeno needed them, their outfits were light.

Making the britches for the men was MUCH more fun, they had to be carefully fitted. Two skins for each leg, one seam going up one leg and down the other, and one seam in back, the front part lapped over, tying on the side. The garments were basic and they could alter them themselves. The women could make four sets of britches in a day.

The smoky smell of buckskin was soothing to Madora, **Loula liked it too…** Loula had given her some special tea and flat bread to settle her stomach. Everyone snacked on dry meat and berries, the smell of buffalo soup was in the air. The first pair of rhino hide foot coverings was completed. Dora put on one and Flora put on the other, they strutted about proudly, their feet were comfortable and warm! The braided rhino hair was pretty and very strong.

Lynden was making flat bread on round stones, the result was cups which held soup if you drank quickly. Before they were ready to eat, Thelsie would throw small pieces of dough into the soup, *soup bread,* they were good!

Annee cut Tug's stitches and pulled them out, his fur was growing back, he was just fine. The swelling in Tellaro's eye was gone, he looked like he was winking now. He caught glimpses of the others smiling at him. He was happy his eye was closed. The cold wind went right into his head.

Patrel and Neosha had taken turns watching the big animals on the plains. They hadn't come closer, they seemed to be moving very slowly back and forth. They were still far away. Behind them, the horizon was getting dark and gray, the air had the breath of coming snow.

Patrel thought…. He and Neosha should go to the carcass of the giant buffalo that took Tellaro's eye. The head would look good with the bear and rhinos, it wasn't far. They had taken nothing of the bison that day, he only thought about getting Tellaro back to the dwelling. They should do it before it snowed…. They could walk in their new foot coverings!

Chapter Six

The cold, dry wind had finally quit blowing, Zeno opened the tiny hole in the door to see outside. It looked sunny and cold, small dirty snow drifts were piled up against the poles they had left outside. Tug was making his funny sounds, something between a lion and crow. Zeno noticed the pup was getting heavier as he held him up to the hole in the door. Tug grabbed on to the wood with his claws as he looked out...more sounds....the men came over and took turns looking out. Zeno went outside in his new foot coverings and buckskin outfit, a good day to test them. As he opened the door, Tug sprang out, ran across the clearing to the field where big birds were scratching through the snow and exposed dirt. He didn't creep up, leap up, or sneak up, he jumped right into the middle of them...such a commotion, the birds were squawking, square looking feathers were flying around, the birds ran off in every direction, almost too fat to fly. Everyone came out to see what was happening....he GOT one!

It was three times his size, he was dragging it back to the dwelling by its ugly red neck, it was still squirming and making muffled noises. Tug made a sudden jerk and the bird was silent. He began prancing back now, the astounded group was cheering!!! Tug the hunter, his first kill! When they were finally able to pry his jaws loose, they chopped the birds head off, gutted it, and hung it outside. They got a huge cooking pot and took it to the pond. A hard crust of ice and dirt had formed over the small pond and a light crust of ice covered the big pond, the water was still flowing from the falls but a thin layer of ice covered that too.

They tied the tether to the pot and filled it with ice and water and pulled it back to the dwelling, they were planning a celebration for Tug! When the water was hot enough to scald the huge bird, Booda dropped it in, and the feathers came out easily. Booda laced it to the two cooking poles towards the side of the hearth. He took a long curved sliver of a broken vessel and tied it under the bird to catch the drippings. Then he took wet wooden planks and covered that part of the hearth. It would cook through the night.

The animals that had been on the horizon had moved much closer, they were by the frozen animal heads now. Oscaro and Neosha had been watching them. Tellaro and Petrel joined them and they decided to take a closer look testing of course their new foot coverings and garments of buckskin. Their feet were warmer than they ever thought possible and their steps were springy.

There were five huge hairy animals with humps like the grizzly bear. Enormous tusks grew down from their heads and curved together in front. A tail grew from their faces and there was a big bump on their head with tiny ears. Their backs sloped down to their hips making them look out of balance with another tail in back. They were slowly clearing the dirty snow off the grass with their huge tusks by swinging them from side to side. They would use the tails on their faces to pluck up clumps of grass and put them in their mouths. Maybe it was a nose, no matter what it was, the others wouldn't believe them. They were as big as three bears standing on three fat rhinos stacked up.

One of the creatures lifted up its head and made some kind of blasting sound, the men jumped. Was it a warning or greeting? The creatures slowly turned to look at the men. They gently stepped in front of the youngster. They certainly weren't afraid of them, anything that size wouldn't be afraid of anything. They weren't predators, they seemed gentle, but what were they? *They had to get back to tell the others.*

Jimi was very interested in what they said. Where did they come from, and were there more? He told them not to kill them even if they could. Their meat cache is full!

That night there was a huge halo around the moon. It was so big and so very beautiful. Loula had everyone dress in their new garments to greet it! They could test their new foot coverings, too. It was cold but their feet were warm. It must be some message from the Great Spirit. It was an omen of coming change. Loula said it was a *good* omen, everyone was happy…

Thelsie saw the big bird flying higher and higher with Tug. His legs were running in the air and his whining was getting farther and farther away.

She awoke with a start. That dream kept coming to her every day since the eagle took Tug. She knew why. Winters ago, she took her son to get water at the pool. She had put the tether on the bowl to pull it back to the dwelling instead of tying it to him. While she filled the bowl with water, her son disappeared. He was never found. She hadn't believed a bird could lift a child that large, but maybe that *is* what happened. Tug was whining by the entry door, why?

They had visitors…. The huge creatures came up the trail into their outside work area. The group could feel the weight of their bodies through the floor as the as they passed the entryway. Through the little hole in the door, they could see their furry legs as they meandered by. They bravely opened the door a crack and everyone tried to look out at the same time. Godaleda held Tug and could feel his chest thumping, but he made no noise. The creatures were taking a good look around the settlement, they inspected things with their long noses. The biggest one was black with white streaks, it broke the ice of the pond with one massive tusk. They each took a turn drinking the frigid water. They would suck it into their noses and squirt the water into their mouths. Some of the men had come completely out of the dwelling to watch, the others were squeezed in the doorway trying to see. No one felt the cold. They smelled like the horses of the migration. The animals walked very carefully to each cold fire hole. Their long noses expanded and sniffed the edges. They picked up the long poles they had left outside and with the fingers on their noses, they picked up the tether. The largest one extended its nose and examined the wood plugging the holes in the window slits. Their nose fingers went over the edges of the bear skin covering the relief area. They seemed to be as curious about the settlement as the group was about them. The big eyes of the creatures looked right at them through their thick eyelashes as they started back down the trail with their real tails swaying between their massive hips.

The youngster walked in the middle holding the tail of the large brown creature with the fingers on its trunk! They left the people of the settlement with the most wonderful experience they had ever had together. ***The ringed moon was a good omen!***

Patrel and Neosha started gathering up their trade goods for their trip to the settlement of the Green Bead. Although it was really cold outside, it was safe to travel in winter when the bears were sleeping in their cozy dens. The big cats usually followed the migration. They REALLY wanted to go to the next settlement to tell about them the rhino and bear fight and the new huge furry creatures. *Of course they had the claws and rhino hair to trade…*

In their kits, they each had the shavings from Zeno's frame and some sparking stones to make fire, good flint to sharpen their knives if needed and they carried a small pouch of hemlock for really bad injuries. Hemlock was better than being eaten alive by some predator. Those things they kept together in one pouch suspended from their belt next to their knife.

They grinded grain so Thelsie would make them some flat bread the next morning. She would put cooked meat between two flat pieces of dough, cook it on both sides and slip it into intestines, which they tied around their waists. They would have warm food. They also took dried meat cut up with dried berries and nuts. They had wood bowls they used for both eating and drinking Walking in the cold made them very hungry. There wasn't much scavenging in the winter months. There were two shelters between settlements, each a day's walk. When they dressed, they put their new buckskins on first. Their trade goods were wrapped in their sleeping covers and were folded like a pillow and strapped to their back. Over that they wore a loose tunic with a hood, which was tied with a very long rope at their waist. Neosha and Patrel liked to have their foot coverings high to their knees with drawstrings on the legs of their britches to keep the out snow. Their food was warm and easy to reach. Their water bladders were filled. Their arms were free and they could walk very fast.

Tug's turkey was tender and juicy. Boodo knew just what to do. There was another big bowl of water with onions, mushrooms and drippings, waiting for the bones. Tug was having a hard time staying awake for his celebration. He had lived three moons now, the last was the most delicious. He was growing quickly. On his hind legs he was as tall as the matching children.

When they tried to lift him, his feet would stay on the ground and all his skin would go to his head. He was getting real teeth now and huge back teeth. Most of the noises he made were in his sleep. He was gentle with everything except birds. He loved all the people in the group and *foot coverings.* He might even like the new hairy creatures, he hadn't decided. He and the children were all curled up on the foot coverings by the huge hearth. What a day it had been, no one would ever forget it. The furry creatures were so close you could have touched them. Tug's first kill, and the wonderful rhino hide for the foot coverings that would keep their feet warm even while standing still in the cold ***made life good!***

Chapter Seven

Neosha and Patrel were up early the next morning, anxious to get on the trail. They knew the people in the next settlement well, some were relations. Thelese crushed a strand of mushrooms as a gift to Wanalee who did the cooking there in the settlement of the Green Bead. Loula sent a skein of clean rhino hair to Eveon who did their healing. It was perfect for stitching wounds. Tug knew something was happening and he wanted to go, too! Morning was breaking. Patrel and Neosha could see the creatures between the frozen heads and the horizon. *They talked about **NOT** telling anyone about them.* It was easy getting to the shelters, they were both downhill. The route had just a slight dusting of snow showing small animal track. It was still light as they cleared the shelter and made a fire with the dry wood stacked by the entry. They would replace what they used. Four people with packs could fit in easily. The trail followed the mountain range to the river, the plains were on the other side. The shelters entrance faced the mountain side, with rock walls and wood roofs. Patrel and Neosha had both worked on them. They met at the settlement of the Green Bead eight winters before. Patrel wanted to have his own settlement with a trading area. Neosha knew they needed more shelters to expand the route to make it safe. Patrel was from the east, like Jimi, his settlement was on the edge of the moving ice, soon to be crushed. Neosha was from the west, they worked well together. They were about the same build and could carry a load evenly, they had done it many times. Both of them wanted to go west and find the source of the beads that shined like the sun. Neosha's family built their dwelling, but they used mud baked in the hot sun. He had helped build a huge structure for Thelsie to make her large cooking pots. One oven was as big as a shelter. They learned a lot doing it. It took days to make a big pot… It took a whole moon to dry one. He made a drying shelter for her too, the pots had to dry slowly. More were made than needed, some always broke, but they saved the pieces. The real test was getting the finished pot back without breaking it in the cold, *and* it was uphill. They started mixing dry grass with the clay, like his family had when they made their blocks. That made all the difference, the vessels were very strong. They learned how to make green beads

by accident. Their relief area was on part of a clay bed and had been there for many winters. Clay from that spot turned green when baked. They just used it for beads because there wasn't much. Neosha was anxious to see what they had made recently. Neosha and Patrel finely got to the settlement before nightfall on the third day. It was much warmer, they had a little snow. The group was happy to see them, they had news of their own! It would be hard to explain in sign language or their dialect, so they all went down to the river… Three nights before, there was a huge halo around the moon. They knew it was an omen… ***The next morning the river was dry!*** Just this morning, water had started coming down the river ***from the other direction!*** Instead of running west to east, the river had started running east to west. It was just a stream now. *What could have happened?* Eveon was thrilled with the rhino hair, she had something for Loula. Eveon was a beauty to anyone. Her hair was wavy and black, she cut it to her shoulders and pulled it back with two long eagle feathers when doing her healing. Her brown eyes were big with thick dark lashes. She wore her white buckskin tunic loosely to cover her soft rounded shape. Her spirit was beautiful, too. Her soft hands could heal with just a touch, her voice was soothing. Her gift to Loula was a sliver of shiny metal with the tiniest hole in the end. It came from south, very far away. She could make her stitches easier and smaller than possible with the hook. They all tried many times to make a bone needle with a hole. But, they would break when a small hole was drilled or scraped into the end. Now they had a sliver that could pierce the skin. With the tiny hole and the rhino hair, they could make smaller stitches faster! Loula would love it! Wanalee was thankful for the mushrooms. She had used her last ones a long time ago, they didn't grow there. She had something for Thelsie and Jimi! She had gotten some large seeds from one of the traders two winters ago. She had eaten them before, but she had never seen them growing. She had planted them like Jimi planted grain but, they grew too thick. She showed the men her bushes. They were dried up and tangled. It was hard to get the pods out. Jimi would want them, he would know what to do.

Wanalee had 30 winters, 21 in that settlement, she would soon be an elder. She was short with brownish skin and hair which she wore loose or in two braids pulled back in a bun with two eagle feathers like Eveon. She had a round face with an upside down smile and dimples in her cheeks. She had come up from the same area as Eveon, but earlier. Thelsie spent time with Wanalee, they shared many ideas about cooking. Wanalee wanted to go

to the settlement of the yellow bead, but her legs were too short to make the trip. She knew all the men, they loved eating her food! Birds nested there in the river banks, she would take their eggs. She learned to take them quickly and they would make more. She mixed them with fat and ground grain. Her bread wasn't flat, it was big and smelled so good. Her husband ate so much, he got fat and died.

This settlement had free-standing dwellings. Their work area outside was all connected. They had learned how to make really hot fires for baking their clay. They brought up the wet sticky mud from the river to the first room where things were made. They took the finished pieces to the next room to dry. When the clay vessels were *really* dry and there were many, they stacked them in a raised shelter with layers of grass between. A fire was started over re-burned wood and was slowly fed sticks. The fire could be made hotter and hotter with thick dry wood and relief paddies from the animals of the plains.

Air was blown through a long hollow bone through the coals. The air would make the coals hotter and hotter. Finally, they would let the fire go down slowly and then out. The next day they would unpack the oven. Waiting for the next day was the hardest part. When they made the really big pots, they would wait two or three days to unpack the ovens.

There were many ovens of different sizes and shelters in their work area. There were piles of broken vessels. The men were always gathering wood. They didn't have beavers or bears to help them.

Wanalee and her two sons, Kip and Ira did all the cooking. Their meat cache was for dried meat and grain. Sometimes there were thirty people there. This winter they had twenty. Traders and hunters would come in summer *and* winter. Two traders, Codesky and Wawaluka had come down on the river and they were getting ready to walk back to their settlement. They would have to leave their wonderful canoe and most of their trade goods. It was three moons to walk. They had loaded their canoe with salt from the endless water and had planned to go farther west. They had gotten what they wanted already, beautiful feathers from far south. They could carry them back in long quivers.

Wanalee's hearth was big enough to cook two small deer at the same time. Her sons had made her a stone oven for her bread like the clay ovens. It heated from the bottom. She new just how to make it work, it was always going. The hungry men could hardly get enough of her bread, beans, and the bright red meat of the

antelope. It was Wanalees' delight to have clay bowls to serve them.

After the eating was finished, Ollieoheh the elder greeted all the traders and invited them to get out their trade goods. The smell of bread still lingered in the air. Wondrous things appeared on Wanalee's two long wood tables.

Noesha and Patrel showed their twenty gigantic bear claws and braids of rhino hair. Next to them was a high pile of white buckskin from the settlement of the Pink Bead.

Codesky and Wawaluka had salt and beautiful orange, green and iridescent blue feathers, which came from south of their settlement far away. They both had copper-colored skin and long black hair braided in a line down the back of their heads. Graduated orange feathers were stuck in the sides of the braids framing their faces. Their orange story beads, brown buckskins and skin were breathtaking altogether. The feathers swayed in the air as they turned their heads, it made people dizzy.

The other table was full of the vessels made there. There were three very large vessels for cooking and many bowls of different sizes. They were made by Alocore, he had been there for many winters. He worked with Thelsie and many others making clay items for trade, he had come from south where Godaleda's settlement was.

Patrel and Neosha wanted the canoe. They could go trading faster, that is of course if the river filled up again. They talked about it. They also needed more vessels especially after eating from Wanalees clay bowls. The skins were needed, how nice not to have to tan them.

Everyone was in deep thought...

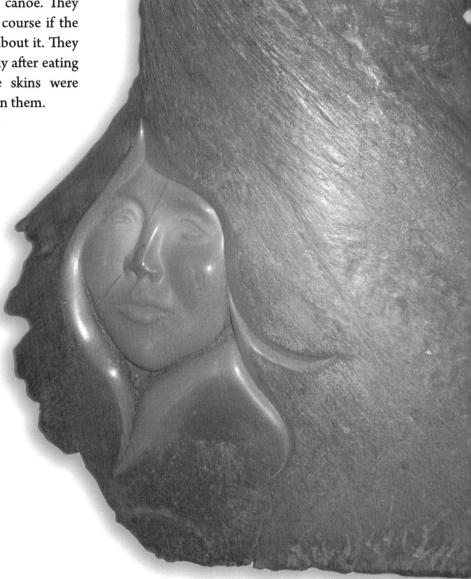

Wanalee

Chapter Eight

Codesky and Wawaluka weren't looking forward to the trip back to their settlement. They could get more salt but the canoe was special. It was fast and had lots of space for trade goods. It had been made from the skin of the biggest crawling creature they had ever seen. They floated in the murky water and looked like green logs… They ate the pink birds and anything else that moved. Their mouths were long and lined with pointed teeth. They could whip their barbed tails and stun or kill other animals… This one lived so long its lower teeth grew up through the top of its mouth. The canoe had been made to fit the skin. It was firm and would glide through the roughest water. They had it three winters. The trip back would take them ten times as long and with their foot coverings, *they might not make it at all.* If they stayed at this settlement, Wawaluka could lose his spirit if the elder Ollieoheh found out how he desired Eveon. Codesky had never seen Wawaluka act so foolishly, however, he could see why. To betray their kindness towards them would be shameful and they would never be welcomed at the settlement of the Green Bead again. Morning was breaking, Codesky was dragging Wawaluka and the packs to the canoe. To their disbelief the riverbed was empty and their canoe had tipped over on its side, high and dry. In a daze, they went down into the empty riverbed. ***Where had the water gone?***

Wawaluka took it as a sign from the Great Spirit that he should stay here at this settlement. There was a chance that he could win the affection of Eveon, his chest began thumping at the thought of her soft... Codesky hit him in the side. The water had started coming in from the east side of the river now, but very slowly....

Codesky wanted the bear claws. Not only were they gigantic, but beautifully finished. One claw would get them a new canoe, the power of the bear would get them safely back to their settlement. Both men wanted the rhino foot coverings worn by Neosha and Patrel but their feet were too big. Maybe next winter they would go to their settlement of the Yellow Bead first.

Wawaluka and Codesky were brothers, Codesky was the oldest and tallest. They looked alike, high cheekbones, eyes wide apart, thick eyebrows and a point of hair on their foreheads. That tip of hair was the beginning of a thick raised braid, which went back across their heads down their backs. The feathers were firmly stuck into the braids, they radiated out making an oval around their faces, looking at them made you dizzy.

They had been trading for a long time. Their settlement was much warmer with many more people. They loved feathers, some had special meaning. They were used for ceremonies. They had gotten some beautiful ones from another trader the day before. They were very long and blue-green iridescent with a spot on top. The trader had special quivers made for them. Neither men had seen any like it before, it would make their trip worthwhile if they could ***just get back.***

The trading started and as was the custom, the new traders, Codesky and Wawaluka would go first. They moved slowly, the tips of their orange feathers shimmered and swayed. They knew none of the dialect but lots of the sign language. Two hands were ten, a tap of a foot was another five, another tap was five more. A tap on the table was twenty.

In the flickering lamp light, a deal was finally struck...five front bear claws for the canoe, five back bear claws for forty bags of salt and feathers. They got ten iridescent blue, twenty orange, and ten green feathers. A gift was made of five braided strands of rhino hair. Chests were throbbing, the agreement was good. Codesky and Wawaluka were relieved and knew they would get back to their settlement.

The bear claws were so desirable, Paluska, from the Pink Bead settlement, offered twenty of the white buckskins for five of the back claws and ten bags of salt. For rhino foot coverings, he offered his help getting all the trade goods back to the settlement for Patrel and Neosha. Paluska had pulled the buckskins from his settlement on a sledge. He was taking some big cooking vessels back to his settlement, but that could wait. He wanted the new foot coverings and had never been to the settlement of the Yellow Bead. He walked long distances quickly and was very strong, he looked to be almost the size of Jimi. He would walk with the sledge harnessed to his shoulders.

Alocore wanted salt. He traded Neosha and Patrel (they had gotten **all** the salt), a big vessel and twenty bowls for ten bags. He was hoping to get it for nothing when Wawaluka and Codesky were stranded. Once, he threw some salt into the oven before he baked his clay. It made shiny places, but it was the salt they used to jerk the deer and antelope. He wanted his own to use. He gifted Neosha and Patel twenty small bowls for the people in their settlement.

Paluska and Alocore had known each other for many winters. Paluska would help gather wood for Alocore's fires and help him move his ovens which were very heavy. Alocore was a short, fat old man now. He wore a shimmering green feather in what was left of his graying hair, a gift from Wawaluka and Codesky. He and Paluska had made some huge vessels for tanning skins. It had made the tanning go quicker. Paluska used salt and animal brains. He would trade the bear claws to the hunters who brought him the skins.

Ollieoheh had a place to store the extra trade goods for the traders, it was by his and Eveon's dwelling. Her healing rooms were on the other side. It was always good to have traders and the hunters. Together, they had all dug a pool to catch the little stream of water in the riverbed. They were always gathering wood and bringing in fresh meat. There had been many men through the settlement, Eveon had healed most of them. They had all desired her but she had never been attracted to any of them until Wawaluka. Though she tried not to show it, Ollieoheh could see a flicker of desire in her eyes, which he hadn't seen in many years.

He had met Eveon when she was young, in the settlement of the Brown Bead. He had twenty-two winters, and she eight. Her father and mother were killed when a fire swept the settlement. They had somehow managed to get to the settlement of the Green Bead and

Paluska

had been together there since. They had a son, Olivee who went missing two winters ago when he was six. The sadness made them closer. Her many tears stained her cheeks.

He felt relieved when Wawaluka and Codesky were leaving. The river... *why would the river run dry and then flow the other way?* They would be leaving again **soon**, he hoped. Wanalee had seen the canoe coming down the river as she collected the eggs in the river bank. It held two men with beautiful orange feathers in their black hair. The feathers shimmered in the morning sun. She ran to the settlement and told the others. They tied a rope from the canoe to a tree stump and pulled the men onto shore. They could see from their story necklaces that they had come from very far south east. One of the men had been injured, he couldn't stand. They all carried him to Eveon's healing room.

Eveon gave him the cup of birch to ease his pain, the men helped him onto the table and left. The lamp's light flashed through the orange feathers as he writhed in pain. She gently removed his buckskins and began looking for the problem. His copper colored body was completely hairless, she hadn't seen that before. He had certainly become a man, it was hard not to notice. She bent his knee and gently lifted his leg up and to the side. She bent his opposite arm at the elbow and pushed it backwards.

With one finger she pushed his shoulder to the side. Every bone in his back crackled. He took a deep breath and the pain left his body. No words were spoken. He lay there, finally breathing with no pain. He looked at her and his chest started thumping, he had no covering and she was the most beautiful woman he had ever seen. She smiled and gave him his buckskins. He gave her the sign of thankfullness and gratitude....

Eveon loved her life in the settlement. Healing people was interesting and rewarding, Ollieoheh was a wonderful man. Although she longed for her son, she couldn't be happier. As she opened the door to the healing room the sun hit two long iridescent green feathers on her work table, *her chest started pounding....*

Eveon

Chapter Nine

Tug was whimpering and sniffing the bottom of the outer entryway. The family of furry creatures had returned for a drink. Everyone put on their new foot coverings and buckskins, it was much colder. Tug was out the door, everyone gasped...The furry creatures were on the trail coming up to the ledge. Tug ran to them and sniffed their huge feet. All their long hairy noses extended and sniffed him as they went by. Tug raced up to the big pond, which was frozen thick now, he knew what they wanted. This time the large creature put its foot down hard on the ice. The huge foot broke through making a large hole. They each took turns drinking the cold, cold water with their noses, Tug did too. No one made a sound, they just watched. The extended trunks inspected Tug, again the small creature's hairy nose touched Tugs nose and *snorted!* The group giggled.

The snow started fluttering as the family of furry creatures ambled back to the plains. Jimi got the cooking vessel and took advantage of the big hole in the pond. He saw the steaming pile of relief from the furry creatures, which was starting to freeze, he wanted it for his grain.

Booda and Kiisco drug out a section of young rhino meat. The cold made them all hungry. Annee was feeling the wall of story necklaces, Thelise asked why. Annee asked her if she saw the new ones. Thelise gave her some peppermint tea *and went for Loula...*

Loula had wanted to go into the cave of the elders. She thought of it every time she tripped over the rhino rope in the hallway. Annee could go with her, they could ask Godaleda to carry a torch for them. Tellaro and Zeno had gone for more wood. Jimi was too tall.

The cave was dark and cold. It smelled musty but intriguing. Loula tied the rhino rope around her waist for a tether. Annee was behind her holding the rope, behind her was Godaleda. She saw the possessions of the man who drank the hemlock. She picked up his pack and passed it down to Godaleda who put it by the entrance of the cave.

The opening of the cave was narrow. The ancient people had used hides to close off the front and again to close off the next opening, which steeped up into a wider room. Huge hides hung over the entryway, though very stiff now, would have sealed the entrance from the cold. The logs they had used and the heavy rocks that

kept the logs from rolling back were still there. There was a barrier to keep out the animals too. It was tipped against the wall. It had been built on the inside of the cave and was too big to take out. The cooking area was on one side, it had a large hearth. The rest of the huge room may have been where they worked, though now it had packs and bundles stacked almost to the top and deeply around the sides. The center of the room was used to store extra things from the dwelling. The smoke from the torch was moving towards the cooking area. Godaleda wondered if the hearth might still work.

They could hear Tug making his strange howling noise, something was happening. They went back quickly taking the pack. Tug was hopping around in circles, sniffing, wagging his tail, and jumping on the door. Neosha and Patrel had returned, how could he know? They were still below the ledge.

Getting back to the settlement with such a big load was hard. Paluska's help and his sledge made it possible. The shelters were a tight fit with such a big man, but they were so tired, it didn't matter. Wanalee gave them some wonderful thick bread and smoked antelope. They stole a big rabbit from a Lynx, which had moved into one of the shelters. They roasted it on the fire. Paluska didn't speak a lot, nor did he sign much. His foot coverings weren't good, the cold would go right through them. Patrel and Neosha took them off and rubbed his feet in the warmth of the fire. They were red and calloused, his toenails were too long, Paluska needed to see Loula and Annee. They felt bad that he had suffered bringing up their load. Patrel cut one of the buckskins in half and made him some temporary foot coverings for the night. Soon Paluska was snoring.

The men could see the smoke pouring out of the side of the mountain as they approached the settlement. Above the dwelling, the moon was rising. As they got closer, they showed Paluska the frozen heads on the horizon. They hadn't told anyone about the family of furry creatures, but Paluska pointed to the fresh huge round tracks going up the trail. ***They had returned!***

When they finally got the load up onto the ledge, they turned and looked across the plains and saw the creatures ambling along near the horizon. Paluska took a good look. By that time, Tug had gotten out the door and was greeting them all. Paluska had never seen an animal like him, either! Patel picked up Tug, his wet tongue nearly froze to his cold face. The smell of roasting rhino drifted out the door, they were hungry!

Annee and Loula took Paluska to the healing room, Tug took his foot coverings almost before they could get them off. Booda brought a big vessel of hot water in to soak his feet. Annee gave him a cup of birch to drink. His feet and hands were dry and deeply cracked. They began rubbing them with bear grease. Zeno came in to look at his feet, too. He came back with two pieces of alder, which he made Paluska stand on and marked his size. They all moved to the cooking area and they soaked his feet adding hotter and hotter water. Though he didn't understand much, he found the group enjoyable.

First, Dora went up to his knee and took his huge calloused hand, then Flora went to his other knee and took his other hand. Paluska thought he was dreaming. They started speaking at the same time, his eyes got bigger and bigger and he kept blinking. Everyone started giggling, they knew he had never seen matching children. They pulled Jimi over and put his hand next to Paluska's. Paluska's were bigger. They pulled a wet foot up and got one of Jimi's feet... Paluska's were bigger! Then they touched his story necklace, how pretty were his pink and black beads.

The rhino roast was ready and everyone was eating from the new clay bowls that Alocore made, and drinking peppermint tea in the small vessels. The salt was good! They were so delighted to have gotten new things. Afterward, Patrel got out the new feathers, they each got an orange one. The stack of soft white buckskin had protected the vessels on Paluska's sledge, they were grateful for the new and wonderful things.

Neosha gave Loula the needle and Jimi got the seed beans. Patrel tried to explain about the river running away and coming back in a different direction. They drew pictures of the canoe on an old piece of skin, another hard thing to explain. Tellaro told them about Tug and the furry creatures.

While they were talking, Paluska looked at the wall of story necklaces. There were so many. He saw they had mostly come from northeast but many other places too. So many spirits left at a young age and many had gone missing. As he looked at the other wall he saw the necklace of the man who ate hemlock, he had known him, it was Coy! He would tell Loula. He saw they used smoke to tan their buckskin, which turns the skins brown, and their outfits were newly made. He saw all the new foot coverings hanging from a bar across the room top, and he saw the pile of old foot coverings Tug was sleeping on, his were there. He couldn't help but smile.

Loula took Paluska back to the healing room, his feet were ready. Annee had more hot water ready for his hands. He sat down, they each took a foot. Loula had freshly flaked stone scrapers that could cut through anything.

Annee showed Loula a bump on the side of Paluska's foot. She said it was another toe growing because he was so big. They removed lots of thick skin on his heels, toes, sides and the bottoms if his feet. They cut off his long toe-nails, which looked more like animal claws, they rubbed the rough edges with pumice. Soon his feet were looking pink and feeling better. They cut his fingernails and wrapped his hands in fat un-scraped animal skin with healing salve. He was very sleepy. When they were done, Paluska made the sign of thankfullness, a fist across his chest. He then took them to the wall of story necklaces. The group, who weren't sleeping already, gathered around.

He pointed to the necklace of the man who drank hemlock. He said in a deep and resonant voice, "Coy". He pointed to himself and made the sign of companion, an arm around someone's shoulders. He thought....

He made the sign of a long toothed cat, two fingers in his mouth...then he bent one finger back trying to show one tooth was broken. He made a sign across his mid section and growled...Tug rolled over and tried to open his eyes. The big man lay on the floor and pulled his tunic up into his fist and pulled it out with the other hand trying to show intestines coming out. He motioned Loula over and took her hands and pushed the tunic down and showed her making stitches in his midsection. He put his fingers to his eyes to show death, but pulled them away quickly! He took Loula's hand and put it to his forehead showing gratitude. The group watched intently. Loula and Annee understood what had happened.

Paluska got up and made the gesture of "what happened"? Loula left and came back with the hemlock bowl and some charcoal. She went to the entryway and knocked, she came in holding her sides showing cold and she shivered. She put charcoal on her feet and hands and face to show frost bite, she hoped he understood. She took the hemlock cup, which had two Xs carved in the side and pretended to drink.

He sat down and was still, water came from his eyes. Jimi took him to his room. The matching children were asleep. Jimi rolled out Paluska's bedding beneath them on a large wooden shelf. He was almost asleep *before* he lay down. Jimi had never seen a man bigger than himself. He admired the harness and sledge, he wanted one.

Sweet rhino stew with mushrooms and onions was bubbling in the new vessel on the hearth. Zeno stuffed Paluska's old foot coverings with rhino wool so he and the others could go outside and collect more wood with his sledge. He also made Tug some foot coverings of his own so he could go. Tug laid on his back and ran in the air with his *own* foot coverings!!

It seemed to be warmer, wind was coming from south, tiny ice crystals were drifting around in the air. All the men were outside inspecting the harness and the construction of the sledge. Tellaro picked Tug up and set him inside the harness...if he were bigger he could pull it, it was a good thought. Tug was growing so quickly now. Zeno said he could make a small one that he could pull. They all went up the trail behind the settlement. Enough snow had reached the forest floor to nearly cover the frozen mushrooms, it looked like little orange circles were scattered through the white snow.

They loaded a lot of wood on the sledge. Paluska pulled, the men pushed it free and steadied the load going down to the dwelling. Jimi, Godaleda and Zeno looked around for more wood to take. He was looking for the right wood. Tug forgot about his foot coverings when he found some tracks in the snow, his first lynx! The snow froze to his wet nose as he sniffed. The men were already back for another load. Three loads were plenty. In hardly any time they were back in the dwelling. They were more careful about leaving things in the outside work area, now that the furry creatures were visiting. They went to the ledge and looked out for them. The horizon was dark, dense fog was moving north over the plains, they were out there, somewhere.

The next morning was much warmer, and so quiet...it had snowed. They pushed part of the entryway open. The snow was light and fluffy. It landed on every branch, every twig, every pine needle, it was so very beautiful, everything looked clean. Everyone wanted to go outside. They used the sledge to clear the snow. They could see the creature family just past the frozen heads. The looked even larger now covered with a thick layer of sparkling snow.

The big creature was clearing the snow off the grass with its' huge tusks. They swayed back and forth...the others were following them along the wide trail. They showed Paluska the winter visitors. He had to be careful returning to his settlement. His white buckskin would be safer, he would blend into the snow.

There were tracks by the frozen pond, too... tracks of the huge cat with big teeth and the big wolf, along with porcupine, lynx, skunk, and turkey. Booda had broken through the ice the same place the creature had before. Now ALL the animals in the forest could have a drink, going outside would be dangerous.

Paluska was giving the matching children a ride on his sledge, he was wishing he could stay. Zeno had made his foot coverings, an extra pair was drying on the wood foot forms. He wished he could do more for the settlement. The women here were nice, not like those in the settlement of the Pink Bead. Olgara and her sister, Doralone were nice to look at, but... Medora asked him to help her get snow to melt, she wanted a lot, the women were going to wash hair next. She had a thought for Paluska. She had been pressing the wooly rhino wool into foot shapes and thought that she could make shapes to cover the ears of the men to fit under their braids when they went out in the cold.

The three tallest men went first, their hair was the longest. Medora used the soap made from ash and fat, Lynden rinsed with peppermint water. They took the soapy water and used it again to bath in the entry room. Kiisco and Booda kept the water coming.

Jimi's hair was striking with his white streaks winding through his loose braids. His eyebrows were dark but his facial hair was thin and white. He relaxed by the hearth with a new clay bowl of rhino stew. Paluska was next, his hair was so thick that Lynden started a three-strand braid by his temple and gathered another strand to pull the braid back. It made a flat braid over his ear, she pulled another strand from the back of his neck. He had two thick, flat, five-strand braids. It looked good and would keep the cold away for his journey home. His dark eyes were sparkling under thick eyebrows.

Tellaro was next, the women had plans for his hair. He usually wore it loose, tied back if he went hunting. Lynden parted it on the side and pulled it loosely over his winking eye. She started a braid at the top of his ear and wove a piece of buckskin into the end for a tie and a feather. He wanted a small orange and green tipped feather from the bird that took Tug up. Loula trimmed the rest of his hair to the end of the braid. It came to his elbows. He looked good, they all giggled. Patrel got the vessel Thelsie had put in their room. They showed him what he looked like in the shiny bottom of the glue pot. He liked it! The men all looked at themselves in the glue pot.

Patrel tried to show the group how Wawaluka and his brother had braided their hair and used the feathers. He tried to braid Oscaro's hair, he made a mess, they all laughed. There was no point in front to start with. Lynden thought something...she made Oscaro lay on the table. With his head hanging back a little, she was able to start a five strand braid. She pulled strands in from the sides. Loula helped her hold them and they made Oscaro sit on a bench to finish.... They ended the braid where his head turned in midway, they wove a piece of buckskin through to tie it off. Feathers could be put there, the rest of his hair would be loose. Loula cut the bottom of his hair in a line right over his waist. They

tried the eagle feathers! He looked good. They did Patrel's hair the same way, so they could show their feathers and make people dizzy. His hair was thicker than Oscaro, he looked good! A thought came to him about the eagle feathers, they were from a different kind of eagle, the green tipped eagle feathers might be desirable to the people of the Green Bead settlement.

Zeno wanted a braid like Tellaro but on both sides. Godaleda wanted his braids loose, starting behind his ears. Booda wanted just one braid in back. He washed his hair more because cooking made it greasy. Kiiscos' hair was thin and some was missing on top. He just wanted it pulled back and tied.

Tug was lying on the foot coverings snoring, but not for long. The women had some hot water left, Tug had his first bath.

Nine clean men sat around the huge hearth eating rhino stew in clay bowls. They were happy and relaxed. Patrel and Oscaro told the group about Wanalees' stone oven and her big bread. Oscaro could build one for Booda. They talked about the big canoe and the river that changed its direction. Their cream colored bodies were lean and healthy. Some had a little facial hair, Paluska and Jimi had hair all over. That night as Tellaro passed the healing room, he called out, "Lulu".....

Nothing was wrong with Tellaro, nothing at all… There was no hearth in the storage room. The warmth of his lean body and being covered in his long clean hair that smelled of peppermint made Loula dizzy… she had missed him…

Chapter Ten

The next morning Tug was whining and pulling on the white buckskins covering Tellaro and Loula to get them up. Jimi was in the relief room with an oil lamp, so was Medora, there on the floor in a pool of blood. Her spirit left her in the night. Annee had seen her necklace on the wall and many more, but she told no one.

Kiisco brought her body to the healing room, Loula sent him away. Annee put the cover over the door. Loula and Annee removed her stained tunic. Her body was hard and white, her arms clutched her middle region as if she was still in pain. Her eyes were squeezed shut. It was hard to straighten her body, but Loula wanted to show Annee where babies were made. She wanted to see what was so wrong with Medora, she had lost seven children. This one didn't come out, they could look inside and see why.

She made a cut down the middle of her slender body. They gently opened it up. They knew her spirit had left in the night, they had no fear.

Loula showed Annee all the parts. Her intestines weren't curled up like Coy, the man who drank hemlock. There wasn't much color. All her blood was on the floor in the relief room. There was a big bulge towards the bottom where the baby was. She cut open the bag holding it and saw what happened. The fluid had come out, but two tiny matching children were still there. Jimi was right, being frightened by the bear caused matching children. When she picked them up to show Annee, she realized they were stuck together down their backs. She backed away from the table and said nothing. Annee's eyes got big. Loula took her hands... she said to say nothing about this, tell the group they were matching children, that is all. Annee agreed. Their chests were throbbing. Loula put them back into the pouch and sewed them back into Medora's body. Water was coming from their eyes.

The men cleaned out one of the outer fire holes and they gathered wood. The women wrapped Medora in one of the new white buckskins, which she would never get to sew. They put her body on the pile of wood and lit a hot fire. They stood around the fire hole playing the drum softly and sung sad songs, she was a good woman.

The smoke from her fire drifted north across the plain. The furry creatures raised their hairy noses and sniffed the air. The smoke drifted farther and turned the snowflakes that had begun to fall into drops of water.

The men drug an elk's shoulder from the meat cache and tied it to the cooking poles in the big hearth. They grinded some grain for Thelise's flat bread. Everyone sat quietly around the hearth drinking peppermint tea. Jimi made a place for Medora's story necklace on the wall. Kiisco held his head in his hands, it was hurting. He got up and asked Loula for some birch but fell over before she got back. His eyes weren't right. The men took him to the healing room, they all crowded the entrance. His body started shaking, Loula got a cover, he shook more and then became very still. He tried hard to breath. Loula put her ear to his chest but heard nothing, she put the two fingers of death on her eyes to show his spirit had gone. The group slipped away from the entrance. No one said a word.

Jimi and Paluska went outside and put more wood on Medora's fire. The men got another white buckskin and wrapped Kiisco's body. They put his body into the fire pit with Medora's. They stood around but could not sing, they played the drums louder, the drops of water coming from the sky were bigger.

The warm rain had melted all the new snow into a thin layer of mud. Water was flowing over the frozen waterfall and draining into the hole the furry creature made. The south wind was blowing harder. If Paluska tried to go back to his settlement now and it turned cold again, he would get wet and freeze. There were things to do. The bear skin covering the relief area was thawing and coming away from the edges. Some how they had to stick it back. Godaleda brought out the rhino rope and drew a plan to lash the bear skin to the relief area with antlers. Zeno said yes it would work... Godaleda, Zeno and Paluska cut some rhino rope and went outside with antler tines. The wind was pulling up the whole back edge of the wet bear skin. More water was flowing over the icy falls, icy chunks of the falls were breaking off and crashing through the top of the pond. The job was done as darkness came. The wind was howling through the trees. They took off their wet clothes in the entryway and warmed themselves by the hearth and drank peppermint tea. The roasted elk smelled good. As they gathered in the eating room, the ice from the waterfall broke free from the cliff and exploded into the pond. They were all thankful for a warm dry place, good food and each other. The day had been hard.

The story necklaces of Medora and Kiisco were on the wall now, they were entwined. It had happened so quickly. The ear warmers Medora was making the night before were still drying by the hearth in the entryway. Losing someone was bad for the group, but two people...in the same day. Tug could feel their sadness, he lay quietly on the foot coverings and shivered for no reason.

That night the wind blew and blew. They could hear it whistling through the edges of the wooden window slots. They could hear the ends of the rhino rope banging against the bear skin which was drying tighter and tighter, it sounded like the drum they played for Medora and Kiisco. They didn't sleep well.

The next day was strangely calm and sunny. The men went outside to check the bear skin, it had held. The waterfall was flowing again, huge chunks of ice were bobbing around in the pond. A warm wind was gently blowing, the ground was muddy. *They were about to have company...* The family of furry creatures was back, **why?** There was snow melt for them to drink, the rhinos were gone. They were at the bottom of the ledge making their way up the muddy trail to the outside work area. Tug was happy, he was whining and sniffing and wagging his tail. The whole group came outside this time. No one was afraid. Annee held the hands of the children. Paluska stood in front of the group in a protective way and the creatures sniffed him like they had Tug as they passed by. They were wet. When they were all up on the outside work area, they did an amazing thing, they started shaking the water of their hairy bodies. The ground shook, the group got splattered and started laughing. Laughing was good. What could those huge furry creatures want?

Chapter Eleven

The wind was coming from north as Wawaluka and Codesky were walking down the empty riverbed, it was frozen. Dead fish littered the banks. The edges of the stream were freezing. The river had flowed the other way for a very long time, the plants, bushes and trees were growing west to east. They seemed to be walking in a dream. A full moon was rising in the east above the mountain. There were some big fish that had been stranded, they could eat them. They made a little shelter with wood and branches in a niche in the wall of the riverbank and started a fire. They caught and ate lots of fish on their trip up to the settlement of the Green Bead though not as big as the ones they could see now.

The wind was blowing harder and harder across the top of the bank, they built a second fire and dug farther into the river wall as it thawed. Why did they leave the settlement of the Green Bead...? Oh yes, the elder Ollieoheh wasn't happy with Wawaluka. Death at his hands would be better than freezing. Codesky was thinking they should go back, so was Wawaluka, but for different reasons. As they sat there by the fire, they saw a huge brownish wolf-like animal jump down into the dry creek and grab a frozen fish. They put more wood into the fire hoping the crackling of the flames would cover up the crunching of the bones in his jaws. When they were sure he had gone, they went out for more wood and branches. It was getting colder, the stream had frozen over but wasn't solid. The sun was setting while they got more fish and stacked layers of wood and branches around their shelter. They knew how to build warm shelters quickly. They had done it for years. The fish cooked and smelled good, but… they were eating the last of the big bread Wanalee had sent with them.

Wawaluka told Codesky the moon with the glowing ring was a sign they should stay there! They wouldn't have to go back at all. They could make a meat cache with all the frozen fish! Codesky said they would have the bear claws and feathers to start their own trading settlement! The wind started howling above them, they put more wood on their fire their teeth chattered as they watched the full moon move slowly across the sky.

The sun was reflecting off the layer of new snow that had fallen during the night. It was warmer! They packed their things and were on their way again. The warmth felt good, they broke through the thinning ice for a drink of the stream water. They would get far that day.

The riverbanks were getting farther apart, this was the place animals crossed. Further down Codesky pointed to a bridge that had been made across the river where it narrowed. They had passed under it on their way. The route to the settlement of the Yellow Bead turned northeast above it. They had been walking for two days and hadn't gotten very far. In their canoe, it was a half day from there to the settlement of the Green Bead.

It was good that the sandy bottom of the river had frozen, their feet weren't getting wet. As they got closer to the bridge, they could see the narrowing had been caused by debris collecting around the bones and antlers of dead animals for many winters.

The bones, wood, sand and dirt were woven tightly together, many animals had drowned trying to cross the river. Wawaluka could see a long toothed cat skull, it was dark with age, the teeth were long and brown. He dug out the skull and loosened the teeth, they weren't heavy. They could get two canoes for them! Codesky had found a skull with a skeleton. It was a man, the story necklace was still there. He took it off very carefully, the cord was old. It was from the settlement of the Green Bead. There were many more. Some skeletons had no story beads, they were brown like the long tooth cat.

They gathered them and put them in their quivers, *twenty-eight altogether.* Nine were green. Six yellow, eight were pink and black, and five necklaces from the settlement of the Blue Bead, where was that?

Suddenly they realized it was getting dark and they hadn't made their shelter. They wanted to stay there and dig more. Dead fish were everywhere, they were limp, they were thawing...it was a LOT warmer. The ground was thawing, they hadn't even noticed. They dug out a niche deeply into the bank and gathered wood and made a fire. They talked about what they should do... If their foot coverings got wet, and it got cold again, they would freeze.

They thought...

Wawaluka took a fish skin and made a foot covering with it. They had lots of fish skins. They formed them over their foot coverings and put them on sticks to dry by the fire. Wawaluka pointed to yellow flashes in the dark....they were being watched. Codesky started throwing the pile of raw skinned fish to the other side of the riverbed. The eyes were gone.

They looked through the story necklaces again, there were so many. They wrapped them in small fish skins and put them back in their quivers. Wawaluka kept looking at the necklace with the blue beads. Codesky got out the blue feathers... They knew where they had to go next...

Chapter Twelve

Wawaluka and Codesky awoke the next morning to flapping wings and screaming birds of every kind and every size. They were everywhere feasting on the smelly dead fish. It was frightening, Codesky and Wawaluka packed up. The fish skin foot coverings were a good thought! The river bed was wet now and their feet were sinking into the sand. They grabbed some big bushy tree limbs to make their way through the flocks of birds.

They worked their way over to the next narrowing of the river where they made a shelter and a fire. Codesky got a bird with his bola, skinned it, and put it on sticks to cook. They threw the dead fish far away from their little site. Too bad these birds didn't have pretty feathers.

They were anxious to dig around. Codesky nudged Wawaluka and made him look up. He was wondering if he remembered the log that was spanning the riverbed. They must have gone OVER it on their way. *Where could all the water have gone??*

One side of the river arched into the middle causing a narrower opening than the last. Codesky's arm shot out to protect Wawaluka from what he was seeing as they got closer. It was a skull as big as a woman with a huge skeleton to match... It looked like the debris was supported *by bones growing up from this gigantic animal's back*. Although the nose was under the sand, the exposed teeth were as big as his forearm. Their chests started throbbing...it was dead, they knew it was dead, but still...

When they started breathing again, they could see that the creature must have died there and its bones strained dead animals and debris trapped in the rivers current. They tried to free the nose from the sand, but it was solid in the ground, it had become a rock. One foot was exposed. It had bony claws twice as big as their bear claws. They measured its body by holding their arms out. Wawaluka touched the creature's nose with his foot and Codesky's hand with his arm outstreached. Then Wawaluka went

to the other side of Codesky and touched his hand and stretched out his arms again. They did it over and over until the bones disappeared under the debris.

What they could see spanned the width of a man seven times. No one would believe them. Codesky looked at the log above them. Was it placed there to view the animal? Had others seen it? They went up the side of the riverbed and crawled down onto the log. It was way below the high water mark. They could see the skull and the huge amount of debris that had collected in the ribs of the skeleton. There

were more skulls and bones from men at the top of the heap.

Wawaluka pried out a black tooth from a skull that too had turned to rock. The bones and teeth were beautifully polished by the action of the river. He took many, they were heavy! Many more brown skeletons of men with no story necklaces were trapped in the debris. One had a necklace of wolf teeth. The cord crumbled when Wawaluka touched it. The teeth were so beautiful. The skeleton had a flaked grey stone knife with a bone handle lying beneath it. Codesky found a group of arrowheads together. They were made from pink and black stone. There were many more interesting things.....but the light was fading and they were hungry.

The bird smelled good cooking, but *tasted like fish*. They wished for some salt and Wanalees big bread. The story necklaces had to be returned.

Codesky told Wawaluka the gigantic creature had made those men dizzy. They fell off the viewing log and became part of his cache of debris, the others must know!

Chapter Thirteen

The furry creatures were changing the front work area. They had pushed down small pine trees from the edge of the forest and dragged them to the ledge forming a ridge or barrier of some sort.

They seemed to have a plan. The group watched in disbelief, but they were grateful for the extra wood. They seemed to be weaving a big basket. The group helped them, they tucked in the branches. Oscaro and Patel picked up the rocks and took them inside to make an oven for Booda so he and Thelese could make big bread.

Paluska watched the furry creatures and thought of how much they were alike.... They were so big, so gentle. Before they knew it was a nose, he thought it was the same part as his...it got bigger and smaller. He so wished he was like the other men. Women were afraid to lay with him, most women.... There were Olgara and her sister Darlone. When he was young, Coy took him to their dwelling so he could become a man. They did things to him, both at once.

It made him feel good for a while, but later he felt dirty. He wanted to scrub their smell off, he had jumped into the river. He hadn't noticed before, but many men went to them, traders and hunters from all over. When the sisters saw him at the settlement, they would call out to him. It would make his face hot, they would laugh. Trading there was good. He could take his tanning vessels and go anywhere there were deer and hunters. He liked the furry creatures, *he would help them build their nest.*

Paluska, Jimi, and Tug followed them up the trail behind the falls. The creatures ate the frozen orange mushrooms! Tug rolled in them, they laughed. Jimi had a thought...he went for a basket and filled it with the mushrooms and took it to the dwelling. He brought the children out to the creature taking care of the youngster. He offered them some in his hand... it gently took them with the fingers on its nose!!! Jimi let the children try, then everyone wanted to feed the creatures! The young creature's nose was soft, his breath was sweet, the matching children got on both sides of it and rubbed his soft fat ears.

The sky was clear as the sun started to go down. The moon was in sight by the cliff. The smell of roasting bear filled the chilly air. The creatures came down from the forest and had a long cold drink by the pond, the ice was bobbing up and down.

That night the group had a good feeling. The furry creatures were gentle, smart and hard working. They wondered how long they would stay.

Patrel and Tellaro took turns watching the creatures. They thought the four big ones were female, the youngster was a male. The oldest was the black one with white streaks and huge tusks… The next biggest was reddish-brown, it also had white streaks, its tusks were big… the two others were younger, probably the light yellow one was the youngster's mother… They all watched out for the little one. They knelt down and rolled on to their sides, with the youngster in the middle, there were sparkles in their hair. It smelled so good outside with pine, mushrooms and the lingering smell of roast bear. There was a chill in the air...

The creatures must have known it was going to get cold, *but how?* The wind from north started blowing, and blowing, it was bitter cold. The rhino cord was hitting the bear hide, they should have cut it off. Wind whistled through the cracks in the window slots. The window plugs shook in the windows. It was the hardest wind they had ever had. They could tell the bear skin was holding, the relief room was quiet. Before the bearskin, the relief room would groan and howl from the holes between the stones. They stuffed little bits of hide into the cracks to stop the tiny blasts of wind that felt like knives. The put hides under the entrance doorway and around the window slots. They cleared a place by the entryway for wood they would bring in the next day. Loula got out the bear grease and they rubbed it into their skin before they went to sleep so they wouldn't itch. Booda had started soup with the bear bones, not just for food, but for the moisture. Jimi added a little more wood to the fires.

The wind had blown all night and was still blowing and howling, but it was light out. Everyone was up trying to look out the hole in the door to see how the furry creatures were doing. They would have to open the door to get wood and they needed to go to the pond for water. They put on two sets of tunics and their new foot coverings. They made a plan... Paluska would open and close the doorway, it was very heavy. Jimi, Booda and Patrel would bring in wood and torches, Tellaro would get ice. They put Tug's foot coverings on, he was excited!!

Paluska opened the door a tiny bit and Tug was outside, he yelled, "Tug"! The wind shoved him up the trail to the frozen pond and slammed him into the cliff wall by the waterfall. Tellaro grabbed the tether and ran after him. Tug was flattened against the wall. Tellaro

wrapped the tether around his own waist and grabbed the pup. He struggled against the wind to the sheltered side of the dwelling and let him relieve. His stream became a vapor in the air. Tellaro glanced at the waterfall, it had frozen sideways against the cliff, he broke off a chunk of ice. The deep pond was frozen and so was the water in the cave floor. There was a mournful howl coming from deep within it. He grabbed Tug up under his other arm and felt the tether being pulled toward the door. The icy blast was freezing his face, he couldn't see. Paluska pulled them through the doorway and closed it.

Tellaro could feel soft hands rubbing bear grease into his face and hands by the hearth. He could see a little, his whole body was aching. Tug was getting rubbed, one of his foot coverings had come off, and his body was stiff, the children were crying. When he could finally move again, Tellaro went to Paluska and gave him the sign of thankfullness, his fist over his chest. Paluska just smiled.

Tug was fine, the men had gotten plenty of wood. The ice was melting in Thelise's pot, a side of buffalo was on the cooking poles. How were the furry creatures?

Chapter Fourteen

Codesky could hear his canoe paddle dipping in and out of the water as he and Wawaluka floated along the lazy river, he could smell the dead fish....

He awoke with a start, it was still dark. The stream was filling with water, it was almost by their shelter! He kicked Wawaluka. The water had reached the fire, it started to sizzle. They packed up and went to the top of the river.... the sun would be up soon. How fast they could move when they had to. They could see the water rising. It covered their fire, it was coming in fast. Where had all the birds gone?

It was cold, the wind was blowing from north, but the ground was dry. They had passed the bridge and were on the migration route going back to the settlement of the Green Bead. At least they would have news for them, **though not good news.**

Vultures were flying around ahead, they were tired of fish and were hoping to find something different to scavenge. But, what they found was horrible...a man who was being eaten by birds!

An arrow had gone through his shoulder. The tip had lodged in his jaw. They shooed off the birds and took a better look... He would have had to walk with his head bent down. The end of the arrows shaft had slots with three stiff white feathers. The settlement of the Orange Bead put two slots of feathers on their shafts.

His story necklace said he was from the settlement of the Brown Bead, there were ten beads there, but he was much older than that, some of his teeth were gone. His tunic and foot coverings had many winters. He had no pack but a short, flaked knife was clutched in his hand. They took his story necklace and carefully pried the knife from his fingers. It was stone from the settlement of the Pink Bead. Where could he have come from in this cold... maybe some animals dragged his body along. They weren't hungry at all after that.

They kept walking, but they did get hungry again, maybe it was because they smelled something very good....it was Wanelee's big bread! They were almost at the settlement. They were sooooo glad to get there. The wind from north was blowing harder and harder. They went first to find the elder Ollieoheh, he was in the steam room by the traders dwelling. They made the room hot with hot rocks and water... it was good for old men like Ollieoheh, the cold made his bones ache. They were finally able to get water from the river... what would they do if it **hadn't** started running again?

They started signing but Ollieoheh took them to Wanalee and sat down with them to eat. Their insides were growling, it was the smell of the big bread. She always had soup going, she was happy to see them. This time their feathers weren't as perky, a few were bent, a few tips had gone missing. The people heard quickly that they had come back. The water in the river had started flowing again, they had no water for a while. They quickly showed Ollieoheh the story necklace and the knife of the dead man, before the others came in. He took it and put it under his tunic...it was a bad thing to kill someone.

Wawaluka brought out the fish skins holding story necklaces and tried to sign between bites of Wanalee's bread, it was sooooo good. They were so thankful to be there, they made the sign of thankfulness many times.

When they were done eating, Ollieoheh gave Codesky a piece of hide and a charcoal stick. He drew a map, but it wasn't good enough. Wawaluka took a big skin from a sitting place and put it on the table and made it the shape of the river. They got two eating sticks to show the bridge and one eating stick for the log. They pulled out the necklaces they had found by the bridge. Codesky asked for another old skin to draw on...he started a picture of the creature.

Wawaluka unrolled the Green Bead necklaces and carefully put them out. The group gathered around and some gasped. He saw the beautiful arm of Eveon slowly reach out and take one, he felt a stab of pain in his chest when he saw the look on her face. She looked at him with water running down her cheeks and gave him a weak sign of thankfulness, and backed away into the darkness of the room. His chest hurt for her sadness. Others came and recognized their relatives. Wanalee cried out when she recognized her Mother's necklace, she had gone missing from the settlement of the Brown Bead many, many winters ago before it burned. She had a small horse tooth amulet in the center of her brown beads, it was blue-white and glowed in the sun. She had found it when she was very young. Her grandfather put the hole through the side so she could wear it. She must have gotten to this settlement!

Two necklaces were claimed by Alocore, who worked with clay.

He **wasn't** happy to see them. They were his wife and daughter.

The six from the Yellow Bead settlement would be returned to them. Paluska would be back soon to go to the settlement of the Pink Bead. Ollieoheh began making spots for them on their wall of missing people. Even with seven filled places, many more were missing.

They found a close match to the very old beads where they started near the top of the wall. There were two strands of green and purple entwined, (man and woman), two others, (their children), then an empty tine, they had a match. Next to them was a long strand of purple and white, green, yellow, green...then three empty tines...three were matching them. Someone had waited a very long time for the return of their family so long ago, how sad...

There were twelve necklaces of blue beads. One had green beads near the top but it was very old. Wawaluka and Codesky made the sign "where", hands out turned up. They wanted to know where that settlement of the Blue Bead was! No one there knew, they hadn't ever seen beads like them before, but they were really pretty. Maybe it had burned like the settlement of the Brown Bead. They could see two green beads at the top of the strand, which meant that person stayed two winters in their settlement. It must have been long ago. Their elder who REALLY knows the stories was very old. He could be the oldest elder in any settlement. His spirit would come and go from his body. His name is Hafpace. His son, Quawlee, an elder also, trapped animals in winter. They had to find the elder...

Codesky had the drawing of the creature's skeleton finished, they would try to explain it. The story necklaces were all taken away. Wawaluka rearranged the big hide. He made the sides of the river bigger and got three logs from the hearth. First he used two small logs for the bridge. He worked the leather into a curve like the creature under the log, and put more leather on top of the log to show it was lower than the bridge. He wanted to know if they had ever seen the log, but they didn't seem to understand. Codesky stood up with the creature picture and moved it under the bridge.

Wawaluka and Codesky got up and showed the group how big the creature was...he put a foot covering for the nose and held his arms out to Codesky' outstretched arms, they did it again and had to go out the entryway to finish showing the seven lengths. The group was amazed.

They all gasped and stepped back, no wonder Wawaluka and Codesky came back. The group all talked together. They wanted to go while the river was low and see!

Time had passed quickly, the wind had started to howl. Wanalee brought more food to those who had stayed to listen. It was bird soup, but hers didn't taste like fish!

Ollieoheh took Wawaluka and Codesky to the dwelling of the traders. They were suddenly tired, a freezing wind was coming from north. There were two traders staying there, Ollieoheh introduced them, they were from the endless waters in the west, Zuggerwulte and Guzz. When he turned to leave, Ollieoheh gave Wawaluka and Codesky his truest sign of thankfullness, which they returned. They were so grateful for a warm dry place to sleep and Wanalee's good food.

The water that was coming from Ollieoheh's eyes froze to his cheeks when he went outside, but he didn't feel it. He felt differently about Wawaluka now, it was a good feeling.

There were wood shelves to sleep on, they had stayed there before. The traders there were tired and almost asleep so they didn't talk. As they threw their sleep coverings out, Codesky saw the traders quiver of arrows by his sleeping shelf. He touched Wawaluka's hand and ever so slightly gestured with two fingers pointed in their direction. Wawaluka only moved his eyes. Nothing more was said or signed, they might understand. They both laid there thinking....

Chapter Fifteen

Godaleda had a thought as he watched Jimi put more wood on the hearths. He motioned to Jimi to come with him into the cave of the elders. Jimi signed that he was too big, but Godaleda said "Come". They took a torch and some wood to build a fire in the hearth. The cave was really cold and quiet. The darkness of the cave seemed thick.

Godaleda tied the tether around Jimi's waist and handed him the torch while he opened the covering to the entryway. Jimi had to bend down, but not for long. They stepped up to a bigger room, Jimi *could* fit. Godaleda had started to clean the hearth when he was there with Annee and Loula. He wanted to know if it still worked and where the smoke went when it was lit. He thought about it a lot. He pulled Jimi closer to the hearth and took his torch. Godaleda soon had a small fire going. The last time it was lit, it was by the elders many moons ago. They watched the smoke go up into a crack at the top of the room. It had been darkened by many fires. The cave started to smell good and was warming quickly.

Jimi took the tether off and tied it to Godaleda's waist. He wanted more wood and could find his way back with the tether, since there was more light from the hearth. The cave was so quiet, no roaring wind, just the crackling of the fire, the warmth felt good. He closed his eyes and thought about what the elders cooked the last time the hearth was lit. It was big enough for a small deer. The space he could see was big enough for fourteen people...he could feel tugging on the tether. Jimi brought more wood and torches, and dry meat, he had always wanted to do this!

Booda wanted to try the new oven...it needed smaller wood that would fit between the stones. He cut some up in the front entry area. The men took turns grinding lots of grain for Thelsie. She knew this would happen...she wanted big bread too, but she needed bubbles. She had thought about it a lot. She had no eggs like Wanalee. There were two things to try...she had soaked some dry berries until they started to bubble. When the children had cleaned the intestines, some water was left and it had started to bubble. She saved the bubbling water in the intestine and added more water and that bubbled, she wanted to try it. It would be nice to have big bread with their buffalo soup.

She poured the bubbling berry water in a new clay bowl with the intestine bubbles and added more water and left it on the warm hearth. She mixed the ground grain with bone marrow and the new salt. She mixed them together and got a big wad, she wished she had watched Wanalee make her big bread.... She turned to the oven...she couldn't just throw it in there...she needed a thin stone to put it on...she called the men in....

They found a thin stone that would work, but it was in the frozen wall. Finally they freed it and filled the hole with a foot covering. *Tug watched...* The stone would fit. She washed it and put rhino grease on top and put it by the hearth to warm. She turned to get the wad of dough and saw it had grown really big and was creeping to the side of the table! It was alive! All of it wouldn't have fit into the oven. The men were watching. She made three sections, and put one on the thin rock. The flames of the oven were leaping up around the door, she put it in.... everyone watched and waited, she was relieved. Booda asked Oscaro if he saw Wanalee's big bread cooking, he was thinking there should be a front cover. Zeno found a piece of wood he wasn't using, it almost fit in the opening, the oven was hot now... they could smell something... the bread was burning... She tried another batch. While they waited, Thelsie mashed the last batch and made little round balls and threw them into the pot of buffalo soup, they got big! That night they all got a little piece of Thelsie's first big bread. The soup bread was good. They all thought of how to make the big oven better.

Alocore

Chapter Sixteen

Alocore thought he shouldn't have claimed the necklaces of his second wife and her child. He was so stunned seeing them, he didn't think. He saw the little clay bird amulet he had made for Bernina, she had liked birds. Who would have remembered...the old elder Hafpace, **he knew**. His spirit would soon leave for good.

That child, she came to him in his sleep through the years. Her high-pitched voice, how he hated it. He would find her hair in his food, even now. He put up with the child because of her mother, but she was nothing, her food was bad, she would tire to quickly when they laid together. She helped him clean, and carry the sticky clay from the river, and she would take care of his son. She would sneak around and use his things, he knew... Even if she could work clay, she would never be as good as him. Four winters with them....

She and her child had come from settlement of the Brown Bead when her daughter had two winters. He had gotten there from way south, the settlement of the Black Bead, with his son. ***His son's mother had gone missing too....***

He had heard from traders about the green clay and wanted to try it. He was angry when it was only green in one area. But, many people there needed his skill, they helped him with the hard work of gathering wood and hauling water. His clay work was known to all the traders, he had value to the people in the settlement. Women would lay with him. He had green eyes that made people dizzy, he looked good when he was younger. Now he was fat, it was Wanalee's good bread. He would make her things, she would lay with him, even now... He still had green eyes. He must find the elder Hafpace....

Wawaluka and Codesky didn't hear the howling wind, nor did they feel the chilling cold until the next morning when the door opened and the traders Guzz and Zuggerwulte, left. Codesky told Wawaluka that they had to find the elder, Hafpace. Wawaluka wondered where the traders were going in this bitter cold.

They asked Wanalee how to find Hafpace. She had bread and soup for him, they would take it for her. They took the blue beads to show him, someone had restrung them with new sinew. The dwelling was far from Wanelee's down by the river. They called out a greeting at the entryway, but heard nothing...the door hadn't been opened in some time. They pushed through. A tiny fire was burning, they needed a lamp or torch, the smell was bad. The elder was there by the fire, not moving. They called out as they came in farther. His head turned slightly, the fire shined through his thin, greasy white hair. Wawaluka put the soup and bread into his hands, he gave the sign of thankfulness. They sat with him by the fire as he slowly ate, their eyes adjusted to the darkness. There were many things in the dwelling, layers of skins on the floor, two sleeping shelves, many packs along the wall, things hanging from the room top, many clay bowls, they saw no water and no son. He had many, many story beads, the most they had ever seen, his necklace went into his lap! They knew he was from west, the settlement of the endless water many years ago, after that were green beads but the light was dim...Wawaluka tried to see, it looked like a blue bead by the green bead. He had tiny slits for eyes, they didn't know if he could see or not. His skin was dark and wrinkled, his tunic had many winters. His foot coverings were falling apart, his long toenails curled to the floor. He motioned for Codesky to put another piece of wood on the fire. His finger nails looked like claws, they were long and curved.

The ancient man looked at them.... young traders from south, he liked the orange feathers in their braids, he leaned to touch one, they shimmered in the firelight. What could they want from him? He made the gesture "what" with his crippled hands.

Codesky gently lifted his story necklace and pointed to his blue bead, he got out the other story necklaces they had found and showed him. He seemed to recognize the longest one, it had a small figure carved in the center, he held it for a long time. Wawaluka and Codesky were sitting closer and closer to him looking for any gesture, but he said nothing and handed the necklaces back. Codesky told Wawaluka to go bring him some water from the river. He grabbed one of the sturdy pots and went out the entryway. Codesky pointed to one of the sleeping shelves and made the gesture "what". He was trying to ask about his son... The old man shrugged his shoulders.

Wawaluka looked out at the river, the stream was a lot wider but freezing on the edges, the north wind pushed it to the other side. It was full of dead fish, *he knew that smell.*

As he turned to go back, he could see someone going in the old man's door....

Alocore liked throwing things into the ovens when the clay was cooking, it made interesting patterns. He had to feed the fires with wood. He blew air through a long bone into the coals until they got red hot. Sometimes it took all night,

he would do things while he waited. Spiders were good... he would see how far they would crawl when they were covered in thin wet clay before they burned up. They left squirmy marks on the clay bowls. He tried lots of things, rats, fish, small animals, the larger ones blew up. Bernina had found a little bird. He soaked it in thin green clay. He threw it in the oven as it was heating. The child should have been sleeping but she had been there watching...when the bird started screeching so did she, but not for long. He threw her against the stone wall, her screaming stopped. He cut off her hair and dipped it into the thin green clay and threw it into the oven.

Suddenly, her mother Valita was there. She saw.....he choked her with her own braids. While he was waiting for the ovens to heat up, he laid their bodies out to harden and waited.... he thought of his first wife....

Nelva was so beautiful, white skin, white hair all over and pink eyes. She was so different, so soft. He had wanted a child with her the first day they met. He had sixteen winters, she fourteen. Their child, Vissil was born quickly. There was so much blood, Alocore hated blood. The boy was long and thin, with light yellow hair and brown eyes. He knew she had lain with someone else....

She was so beautiful there holding the child to her, her breasts full of milk. He wanted to keep her face. There was the clay he was using... *he pressed her face into it....*

Valita's face would be good. He worked the clay and fed the fire.

Before dawn he had the bodies wrapped up and drug the bundle to the shallow part of the river. Hafpace was there filling his water vessels... he helped Alocore tie the bundle to a drifting tree. They pushed it into the current and watched it float down the river.

The next morning Alocore had to take care of his son himself.

He had to go to the settlement of the Pink Bead, the girls wanted things he couldn't send with a trader. He took his son Vissil, he had eight winters.

There were two girls, Olgara and Darlone. They were very friendly. He made things for them, which they would trade for things they needed. They wanted bowls, vessels and Dos. It was their own thought. Dos were shaped like a man ready to lay with someone. It was his shape, of course, to start. He made them very smooth and shiny, as long as a woman's hand. They asked for larger and larger Dos through the years. They showed him how they were used.... *every time he went over.*

He left Vissil with a couple who couldn't have children of their own. He didn't want to take care of a child not his own. He thought Vissil would look good when he got older, but no. He was thin and sickly and didn't see things right. He couldn't learn his colors. He could learn to cook, that would be good....

Chapter Seventeen

Codesky watched the expression on the elder's face change from happiness to fear as Alocore came in the door. He was surprised to see Codesky sitting by the old man, his spirit was with him. What could the old man have said...? Codesky stood up, he was much taller than Alocore... Wawaluka came in the door with the water, there was a strange feeling in the room. He went to stand by his brother. The elder raised his hand gesturing the brothers to stay... Alocore turned and left with stiff knees, he was angry. Wawaluka was about to ask Codesky what happened as the door opened and Hafpace's son, Quawlee came in... He was happy to see his father with his spirit. He spoke in their dialect and signed at the same time so the men could understand... He had been hunting and was caught in the cold wind, but he had a fat deer for Wanalee and some good rabbits they could cook on their hearth. Codesky gifted the elder a beautiful blue feather and they moved toward the door. Ever so slightly, Wawaluka touched Codesky's arm. Codesky followed his gaze to the quiver of arrows by the door, they had three grooves of feathers. Before they went back to their dwelling, Wawaluka took Codesky to the river, they picked up wood for the elder and came back for more wood for the dwelling of the traders. Alocore was watching them, they could feel his green eyes....

The traders hadn't returned, they piled the wood by the door and put a few pieces on the fire, they needed to talk. Codesky said they should take Ollieoheh to the dead man, they could get the arrow. Wawaluka wondered if he couldn't remember how cold it was out there, but he was right, the animals would scatter the bones. They should go soon.

Ollieoheh had the same thought... he was at their door. They went to Wanalee for some food and a big skin. Wawaluka had a strange feeling leaving their packs. They left them in the room by Eveon's medicine dwelling, she was there... Wawaluka's chest was thumping but he only greeted her, and gave the sign of thankfullness.

The dead man wasn't far, but it was bitter cold, their faces had no feeling in the blowing wind. The birds had picked more pieces from the man until he froze. The arrow was there in his jaw. They were too cold to look more, it would soon be dark. They carried what was left of the man rolled up in a large skin. Ollieohh

put the small bundle in the room for traders. The smell of roasting deer and Wanalee's big bread filled the night air.

Wanalee was making a batch of bread dough, she loved making it, the smell was so good. She thought of the clay vessel she had found. She wanted to press the dough into the bottom, she would when she had more time... all these men needed food, it was cold and they ate more.

Wanalee was the first to realize the riverbed was empty. She would gather her eggs from the nests early, before dawn. That morning she was half asleep when she got there. She thought she was in a dream. She could see the edge of the clay bank where it turned to stone. The birds would dig holes in the clay and make nests and lay their eggs. She would gather them and they would make more! It would be the last time, the birds had gone. She reached into the nests and noticed the holes were going down further and lower into the stone leading her to an EMPTY river. The stone nests were full of water, her eyes opened up... She could see footprints of birds with big feet, **really** big feet. Two of her feet would fit into one of the big ones… She got a chill and started to back away. She was standing in nearly frozen mud at the bottom of the empty river, she looked both ways, dawn was coming, and it was lighter... She saw something else... it was a clay pot that was holding icy water.

Many winters ago, when Alocore first came to their settlement she had seen him throw one into the river early one morning when she was gathering eggs. She thought it was an offering to the spirits. She was watching him because he looked good, he made her dizzy. That had to be the pot....

She lifted it up, it wasn't broken. As she looked down, she saw the impression it had made in the sticky, sandy clay. There was a face in the cold mud, it came from the bottom of the vessel. She turned it over, it was beautiful. Why would he offer the spirits something so wonderful?

She covered the impression over with wood and stones. She filled the vessel with eggs, no one would know she took his offering.

Her thoughts were racing...she had seen Alocore walking in the empty river breaking up shards with a stone, there were many broken pieces there, **many**. Ancient people had lived there winters ago. There were shards from them when she came, many old tools too. They were the men with brown bones that Codesky and Wawaluka had found, before people started wearing story necklaces. It was the sticky clay in the river. It was good and easy to use. If you made a fire on the clay bank, it would make the clay hard. You could lift up the whole fire site after it cooled and could move it to a different place.

Her sons helped her with the hard work, getting wood and water. Why did the river dry up? She hadn't heard of any river loosing it's water like that. If it hadn't come back, they would have to move the settlement, but where?

There was lots of wood in the empty river now, maybe the new traders went to collect it. They would be back soon, it was too cold to be outside. Everyone came to her for dried meat and bread to take on trips, even short ones. There was always a lot. She mixed it with nuts and dried berries. She knew all their plans. Eighteen people in the settlement, but not all of them came to her to eat. They had their own hearths, but she was always ready. If she had extra food, she made soup. She was grateful for the crushed mushrooms Thelsie sent. They were so good. It just took a tiny bit. Everyone loved her big bread... she had made it so often, it was quick for her. Everyone could smell it cooking and would come to her tables and talk and eat. Her sons had made her oven like Alocors' clay oven, she loved it. *How could she move her oven to a new settlement?* She was thankful when water came back into the river even though it was from a different direction. **How** *could that be?* Her second batch of big bread was done, the men would be here soon.

Her bread was best with eggs, she needed many. There was a way to have eggs in winter... Once, she had gathered some and forgot them. They were near the oven, and one morning she heard chirping in her cooking area! She kept the chicks outside but they grew big and flew away. Her sons could make a special dwelling for them, they would make eggs for her in the cold winter months, *maybe…*

Having the traders and hunters come was good, she heard many stories about places far away. The hunters would bring her different kinds of animals. She had learned a lot. There was a huge cache for meat. She had many of Alocore's large clay pots, bowls and cups. Her sons had made a special shelf for them. He would bring her gifts when he wanted more than bread. She liked the gifts, but he frightened her. Sometimes he would bring a "Do"... She had seen one made of stone, but it was too big. Someone said it was for women who were *unfaithful.* She was relieved to see the "Do" was for him.

Chapter Eighteen

Zuggerwulte was really sorry he had made that sign to Guzz when he said he wanted to go back to the settlement of the Pink Bead to see Darlone. He signed that she had a big hole and had used *two hands.* Guzz hadn't signed, spoken, or looked at him for a whole day. Now, they were on the migration route in the coldest of cold, he wanted to go back. They had to find shelter. Things were blowing by them, his frozen ears might break off. He thumped Guzz and pointed to the river, at least they would be out of the wind.

The water level of the river was low, and the top was frozen. There were places in the bank they could build a fire. Finally out of the wind, they built two fires and piled up wood and branches around them. Guzz made a barrier between them. Zuggerwulte would go back with or without him the next day.

They pulled their sleeping covers up tightly around them, Guzz wrapped up, put his hands around his legs and rested his forehead on his knees and shivered. Zuggerwulte listened to the river cracking as it froze. The moonlight made the landscape eerie looking...dead fish that had bobbed up and down were now frozen in place. The wind howled across the river above them. He reminded Guzz of their past life on the edge of the endless water. They knew when they were children, they would be traders someday. They collected beautiful pearls and shells from the sand and brought only the best with them to trade. The sun shined in them, even in firelight. Zuggerwulte told Guzz they hadn't taken time to show the people of the Green Bead their trade goods, they just ate and slept there. He would have kicked Guzz if there had been no barrier... they hadn't even brought water and wood for the settlement. Zuggerwulte talked himself to sleep. The wind kept blowing, it felt like sharp stone flakes when it touched their skin.

The hard frozen river ice reflected the morning sun into Zuggerwulte's tiny eyes. His mouth was frozen to his tunic sleeve, he was covered with a layer of frost...so was Guzz.

But... Guzz's eyes didn't open. He was still holding his stiff legs with his icy arms, his spirit had left early that night. Water came from Zuggerwulte's eyes and froze to his cheeks.

He tied his belt to Guzz's sleeping covers and pulled him back to the settlement of the Green Bead on the frozen river. He couldn't feel the cold wind, he wasn't hungry or sleepy, and he hardly remembered getting to the settlement. He passed Alocore's dwelling and the dwelling of the Hafpace and his son. Wanalee had been looking for them to come to her. She brought him in, wrapped him in warm skins and put him by the hearth. She found Ollieoheh, he took Guzz's body to the place the traders kept their things. He was still frozen hard in his sitting position with his head on his knees. They put him sitting up against the wall by the body of the dead man...

Quawlee went to the dwelling of the traders and called to Wawaluka and Codesky. He signed that his father, Hafpace had something for them, but he wanted something in return. They were surprised and happy! They saw the bodies when they got their packs, *how easily* **they** *could have frozen out there...*

The dwelling of Hafpace and his son smelled like roasted rabbit, much better than the day before.... things were arranged for visitors. They had good tea, Wawaluka wondered where it came from. They eagerly sat down by Hafpace and put both hands out with palms up, to start the trade. Hafpace had a piece of birch carved into a map, not freshly carved, but very old. A hole was in the middle near the top. A leather strip was knotted above the hole. The knot was covered by a big blue-green bead, it was a map to wear! The elder knew what they wanted, but what did HE want? They started to get their trade goods but Hafpace put his hands out to stop them. He pointed to the map around his neck and said "Alocore" and put the two fingers of death over his eyes....

Wawaluka and Codesky both sat back at the same time, like they had been hit with a log. They sat in stunned silence and made no moves......

When his senses returned, Codesky put his hand on the old mans hand. Shaking his head, and then, with both hands, he signed "No." Codesky made the sign of fear, two arms crossed in front of his face, and pointed to Hafpace and said, "Alocore." Hafpace closed his tiny eyes and nodded. Wawaluka signed "speak" and said "Ollieoheh"? Hafpace shook his head no… Codesky pointed to his son and asked "Quawlee"? Hafpace made the sign of fear… So, they were both afraid of Alocore, they wondered why.

As Codesky opened the door to leave, the smell of Wanelee's big bread flooded into the room. Wawaluka made the motion that all of them should go eat. Hafpace rose up but they could see his legs didn't work, Quawlee rushed to help him. Wawaluka and Codesky felt bad....

They went back to the traders dwelling to see about Zugerwulte, they laughed about his name. The sun was setting and it was getting even colder. Zuggerwulte was there staring into the fire, looking bad. But, the smell of bread made all their stomachs growl. Wanalee made a special place for him by the hearth. Wawaluka and Codesky sat on each side. The smell of deer soup with mushrooms and wild rice filled the air. Zuggerwulte finally ate and drank birch tea.

Eveon emerged from the shadow and stood behind Zuggerwulte. She crossed his arms and put them across his chest. She put her hands on his temples and pulled the sadness from his head, down his neck, across his shoulders, down his arms and out through his hands and into the air. It floated slowly into the hearth and out into the night. He had been trying to hold onto Guzz's spirit. With her knuckles, she raised the corners of his mouth into a smile. He was looking much better…. Eveon melted back into the shadows.

Wawaluka and Codesky were dizzy watching. They gave the sign of thankfullness to Wanalee and took Zuggerwulte back to the dwelling of the traders. It was bitter cold but the fresh air was good. Part of the moon was out and they went to the river to get wood for Wanalee, Eveon and Hafpace. They all slept well that night.

But, Alocore didn't… He never looked into Eveon's eyes. Although she was beautiful, he knew she could see his thoughts. He knew Wanalee had found the pot with Nelva's face which he had thrown into the river so many years ago. He couldn't bear to break it, he couldn't even bear to destroy the image it left in the river. What could she know, she wouldn't think it was a real person. The water would dissolve the image when the river rose again. He had found most of the others, they were easy to break. He smashed the pot with the child's face into pieces. Her hair was in his food that night….

Hafpace had his spirit now, how could he live so long? **The next dark night would be his last….**

Hafpace had secrets of his own… he wanted *all* of his spirit to leave then he wouldn't have to think about the terrible things he'd done. Hafpace thought more about the Great Spirit as he got older and older… He was so close now, he could whisper Alocore's secrets to Him and maybe his spirit wouldn't turn to dirt. He knew some spirits stayed… He could see the spirit of Bernina, the child of Alocore, by the river catching birds. Her spirit would go in and out of Alocore's dwelling every day. How wonderful that would be, floating around with no pain, no needs, just floating…

He wanted to find the settlement of the Blue Bead, everyone did. Many winters ago, before he met his wife, he met some travelers on the trade route from west. They had blue beads, but not for long. He stayed the night with them in a shelter. He had their beads the next morning. It was simple, he had a sweet tea that made people very sleepy. Then very dead. He dragged the bodies into the woods, the animals ate them… He would take the beads and restring them before he got to the next settlement. He could be from anywhere, though he never found out where the settlement of the blue bead was. Oh well… he just wanted the beads… He traded the beads and other things. Women liked the beads a lot… When he ran out, he just got on the trade route and got more.

One man had a beautiful necklace with many large blue beads.

It had a carved amulet that matched one in the center of the blue bead necklace Wawaluka and Codesky had found. He found the carved map with the blue bead *after* he had killed that man, it was under his tunic…

Somehow Hafpace found his way to the settlement of the Black Bead. He met a girl there, Liti, when he had twenty-four winters. She was beautiful and adored him. They had a son, Quawlee, and for many winters, he had happiness. That is, until his wife's sister came to the settlement with her a child whose name was *Alocore*. He and Quawlee spent time together.

One day they found all the story necklaces he had hidden in the sleeping room. They wore many at the same time and went *outside the dwelling…..* He beat them both until his wife stopped him…they moved then, to the settlement of the Pink Bead. They were finally happy again. He liked chipping out the pink stone. His wife was going to have another child but, they both died.

He took another wife, Pueda who had two daughters, Olgara and Darlone. They all liked beads, lots of beads. They liked men the same way, *lots of them.* They were soon able to get their own beads. Pueda got a strange sickness. She got many runny sores and she smelled bad. She became very ugly and angry. That was before the medicine woman, Tahecha had found healing salve. Hafpace left her with the daughters and took Quawlee to the settlement of the Green Bead.

The only dwelling that was empty was next to **Alocore….**

Chapter Nineteen

Tug knew the healing room well, this time it was his nose. He had pulled the foot covering from the hole left when the men took the stone for Thelsie. His wet nose had frozen against the icy rock. They tried not to laugh at his pain, but it was funny. The skin from the top of his nose was still frozen to the stone.... at least he could finally see outside without someone lifting him up to the little hole in the door, he was getting heavy. They stuffed it with a piece of old hide after that, not foot coverings.

Tellaro looked out of Tug's hole in the wall, he was eye level sitting down... Tug had to hop up to see, the children could stand and see out at the same time. What they saw was the huge pile of furry creatures outside. It was too cold to look for too long but there they were.... Tellaro noticed that their hairy fur hadn't frosted up, they were like the wolverine. No wonder they built the lair, they wondered if they were still alive. It was so cold, ice covered the inside walls hit by the wind, finally the whistling had stopped. Icicles poured from the window slots down the walls. The big bladder for men in the relief room was frozen solid. The cave of the elders was the warmest place. They felt the warmth drawn down the hallway to Tug's hole when it was open. The elders' hearth worked well with little wood but they didn't know where the smoke went, they wanted to know.

Jimi had found places to put the torches. With more light, they looked around the room. Packs went from the floor to the wall tops, there were other things...large tools, long round sticks probably spear shafts, unfinished arrows, stacks of scrap leather, rawhide, rope of some sort. There was much more... There was another opening behind the packs, but it could wait.

It was hard to begin. There were so many... Would looking through these things bring their spirits back to the cave? Why were they doing this? Is it the right thing to do?

Jimi said they would learn much. They could use some of the things for trade goods...there were probably trade goods in the packs. They decided to go through them one at a time and put the things back until they could decide. There was a large tabletop with four short fat legs and four tall fat legs. The short legs were for eating. They used the long legs to make it high for a work table.

Godaleda could see much thought had gone into the interior of the cave... large niches had been carved into the soft sandy limestone places between the hard layers of stone. Those places were used for storage. Some of the stone had been knocked away to leave a thick stone shelf by the hearth. There were antler tines in the wall for hanging things. It looked like the beginning of the story necklaces. There were many, many packs, some were made of leather, raw skins, bark, and wood. They put Medora and Kiisco's things by the hearth, among them were their new rhino foot covering. They couldn't look, it was too sad. Jimi could see his wife's pack buried under the others, water came to his eyes. The deliciously sweet smell of roasting rhino drifted into the cave. They put a few more pieces of wood into the hearth and followed their noses. Thelsie was trying more big bread, it smelled good!

As they ate from the new clay bowls, they talked about the furry creatures. If they were dead, it would be a bad thing. Five of them... Their meat cache was full. The children started crying. They skipped the rest.

There was something different about Lynden...she was looking more like a woman than a girl. She had pretty reddish-brown hair. She had freckles across her nose and had long thin legs. She had fifteen winters, she should be looking for a husband, and not from the Yellow Bead settlement...she knew all those men too well. She wanted someone from far away, like from the settlement of the Endless Water, wherever that was. Some place warmer and with not so much work to do. Now that they had clay bowls, they had to be washed, that meant getting even more water. She liked making food. The new oven could be used for meat as well as bread but Booda didn't think so. He would never let her do what she wanted, she really wanted to leave this place, maybe not in the cold, later maybe. The new salt was good, very different than what they had been using, it was finer. She thought about it as she got more ice to melt for the bone soup and peppermint tea.

Tellaro could hear the echo coming from deep in the blackness of the frozen cave behind the waterfall. He could hear Tug's whines and funny roar and the children's laughter echoing, echoing, echoing...

He woke right up and went to the relief room. A warm draft was coming down the dark hallway. The wind had finally stopped and everyone got a good night's sleep. He could still hear the echoes... Tug and the children were crowded around the hole in the wall... He silently entered the area to see what was so funny. He covered his mouth not wanting to let

out a giggle, left and got the others. He woke them up gently and led them to the entryway.

Darting through the hole in the wall was the nose of the young furry creature. The children would laugh and almost the same sound would come from the creature...Tug would whine, it would whine, he would howl, the furry creature would howl... The group all tried to hold back their laughter...the children would giggle, it would giggle. They had the basket of mushrooms and were feeding it through the little hole. Booda signed that it probably wanted water and went for some, the others watched the happiness in the room.

They could see the sun outside...Tellaro slipped over to the hole in the door. He could hear the furry creatures snoring and could see four vapor lines going straight up. They finally understood why the furry creatures had made such a high barrier, it was for the little one. It was still extremely cold out there, sun or not. The entryway door was frozen closed. Jimi didn't want to scare the creature by chopping the ice away, nor did he want to wake the big ones...they could go outside through the door in the relief room. They got their rhino foot coverings, double tunics and Tug's new harness. Finally, they got outside for fresh air!!!

Booda slipped out with a bowl of water for the little furry creature so his nose wouldn't freeze to the stone, ice was forming on the edges of the bowl. The creature explored Booda's hands and face with his long furry nose. He took a big drink of water and sprayed it into his mouth, Booda could see little tusks starting! He rubbed his ears like he would Tug, the creature leaned towards him for more. His skin was soft and fat but totally covered with a dense layer of wool like the rhino but with long wavy hair the same color as Tug. Under the long thick eyelashes were eyes that twinkled… his long nose was completely covered with thick, fine, light-colored hair. He smelled good, like horses.

Dora and Flora were giggling, they went to Paluska and each took one of his huge hands…. The furry creature made them think of Paluska, they wanted to share his name with it. They wanted to call it, "Uuka". Paluska laughed until water came from his eyes, the others laughed too. It was a good name for the little creature.

Tellaro could hardly get Tug's foot coverings on, he was so anxious to go… Zeno put on his new harness, it was a good thought! Tellaro tied Tug to the tether for relief and to visit with the creature… his tail was going so fast…

The furry creature liked Tug, *his* tail was going back and forth… He sniffed Tug's foot coverings and harness, Tug sniffed his feet, he had rounded toes with thick pads and funny toenails. Suddenly, movement came from the pile of furry creatures, and a low whine… The young creature turned but looked again at Tug before he crawled back into the little space to the warmth of the huge furry creatures.

It was cold, Godaleda took Tug inside, breathing hurt his chest. The men were making a plan to go into the cave… it was like the spirits had made an entryway calling to them to come see…it was so beautiful… The cold wind freezing the waterfall to the side of the cliff showed many flashing colors. It might be their only chance to get a torch into the cave, they had to do it! They would all take quick turns…Tellaro and Paluska would go first, they would need extra torches. They would come back and tell the others what they saw, and two more would go… Thelsie had the men bring in rhino meat for the hearth, it was good on cold days, rhino was fat and juicy.

They went outside with two lit torches past the snoring furry creatures to the pond. It was hard frozen, but not flat. There were many frozen ripples from the force of the wind. Paluska got a log, put it across the entry way, and tied one end of the rhino rope to it…he tied the other end to Tellaro's waist. They were thankful for the rhino foot coverings. They both went inside the cave but Paluska stayed on the ledge in front. It was too slick to walk across the frozen water behind the waterfall. Tellaro sat down with his torch and Paluska gave him a little push, that was all it took, he slid to the other side...The two torches were a good thought, they could finally see...icicles were everywhere in the entryway. Tellaro stood up, the cave floor was higher than the frozen water level, he put the torch into the cold black hole...

He could see bones of many animals coated with ice. An icicle went from the top of the cave and dripped onto a pile of skulls on one side. He could see a huge bison skull, as large as the bison that took his eye. He could see a bear skull and other animals he didn't know. On the other side were stacks of bones, so many, also coated with ice. The ice glowed and made reflections in the torch light...it was so very beautiful... He put his torch against the wall on the inside and called out to Paluska to pull him back. His voice echoed in the cave. He gave Paluska the sign of thankfullness...and quickly tied him to the tether. He sat down and Tellaro gave him a little push...

It was breathtaking to see, Paluska's jaw dropped, he leaned forward with the torch. The cave went back more, they both knew because of the deep echo...how did so many animals get in there, the cave opening was so small...He left his torch by the other one and called out in his deep resonant voice, "Tellaro" it was the third word he had spoken. Tellaro pulled him back.

The others had to come....no matter how cold it was, they had to see.

As they came back through the door of the relief area, Tellaro pointed to the piece of rhino rope that was hanging by the stretched bear hide. It had made so much noise when the wind was blowing. They cut it back, *finally.*

The whole group was warming up by the big hearth drinking peppermint tea, enjoying the sweet smell of rhino and talking, singing and thinking about what they had seen.

They had all known there was a cave behind the falls. But the animal skeletons brought up more questions. How did they get in there? If the cave was a meat cache, it was surely hard to get into it…

And, why were the skulls on one side and the rest of the animal on the other side? Maybe ancient people put logs across the pool on the inside of the cave and led the animals over or maybe they drug them across when it was frozen, or what?

Warmed up and ready for more adventure, Tellaro and Paluska grabbed extra torches and went to the cave again. The afternoon sun wasn't warming things up much. The furry creatures were snoring, their snores echoed from depths of the cave. Paluska moved the log into the second part of the cave and tied the tether around Tellaro. They were anxious to see the next part. Tellaro was careful as he climbed over the opening. Paluska held the tether tight in case there was a drop off. They had no outside light, it was *realllly dark*. As Tellaro's eyesight adjusted, his torch lit up a wall of solid fish skeletons stuck in the rock. It was like they were trying to swim out of the cave...*so many*... five more steps and his legs froze... His chest started pounding, he started shaking, water was coming from the skin on his back...he tried to speak but the words stuck in his throat, he heard Paluska calling to him, his deep voice echoed in the cave ***Tellaro, Tellaro, Tellaro***.

Paluska was only seven steps away, he could feel him pulling on the tether. Tellaro couldn't move! The next thing he knew, Paluska was shaking his arms. He gave Paluska the sign of thankfullness over and over...

He wanted to tell Paluska what he saw, but how?

Paluska was thinking maybe he didn't *want* to see what was in there... What could have frightened a fearless hunter like Tellaro?

He had to go in....

Tellaro untied the tether around the log and retied it in the middle so they both were tethered, they could go in together with two torches....

Behind the fish skeletons that covered the wall, there was the skull of a creature so big both Paluska and Jimi could stand in its mouth. Some of the fish on the wall *were* in its mouth... it had rows and rows of flat, pointed teeth, more than they could count, the teeth were going to the front and to the back like grass. Paluska's chest was thumping but somehow he put his hand on one of the teeth, it was bigger than his huge hand. They held up two torches, it looked like the creature had swallowed the wall, fish skeletons were inside its huge ribs... The skeleton went further and further back. They went as far as the tether would let them. The creature was bigger than the ***dwelling*** they lived in. The cave was deeper still, but they had enough.....

It was getting dark and colder. They saw the red sun setting over the plains. It was going down behind a band of black clouds, a storm was coming, and it would warm up and then snow. They could smell the roasting rhino. That night, Paluska was talking with as many words as he had learned, and signing, as he and Tellaro told the others about the fish and giant creature. Loula said the ancient people were making offerings to the creature so it wouldn't leave the cave.

Tellaro knew he would never dangle his feet in the pond again...

Chapter Twenty

There were two ways to get to the settlement of the Pink Bead, cross the bridge on the east side of the Green Bead Settlement or go past the houses of Hafpace and Alocore and cross at the shallow part of the river. There was a shelter midway but it could be done in a day. As Ollieoheh waited for Zuggerwulte to come, he looked at the murdered man and looked at the frozen body of Guzz. The man must have been shot at the shelter and tried to walk over the bridge. If he had been sitting like Guzz, someone could have knelt behind him and shot his arrow through his shoulder and it would have stuck in his jaw, or else the man was in a tree when he was shot…it seems like it was a little cold for climbing trees now. He wanted to know if Zuggerwalte had seen him in the Pink Bead settlement.

Wawaluka and Codesky went with Zuggerwulte, they knew it would be hard for him to see his friend's body. Food, a good night's sleep and Eveon's help made a huge difference. Zugger woke up signing. He wanted to see their trade goods, he loved the feathers….he showed his shells and pearls. Codesky had never seen pearls with holes, he wanted to know how it was done, how can anyone hold something so tiny and put the hole in…? They were beautiful….

Wawaluka, Codesky and Zuggerwulte walking down the path together, made Zugger look like a child. He had short arms and legs, tiny eyes, a square face, and, he had a brown chin. He wore a pointed hat that connected to his tunic. His story necklace had beautiful pearls and shells that glowed.

They stood by the door of the storage area, Zugger took a deep breath and they went in. The sunshine lit up the cold room. Guzz's body was covered, leaning against the wall by the canoe. Ollieoheh had pulled what was left of the

Zuggerwulte

murdered man into the sunshine, it was worse than they thought… The birds had picked all the meat from the body that the tunic didn't cover, most of the finger bones were gone. His tunic had been white at some time, and his hair was streaked with grey. One foot covering was gone, so were most of the foot and toe bones. Older people usually didn't leave the warmth of a settlement, especially in winter. Ollieoheh thought he might recognize the man with more light, but no. His story necklace had only ten brown beads, but that settlement had burned ten winters ago. Zuggerwulte gasped when he saw him, he tried not to get sick. Zugger remembered seeing him in a shelter before the settlement of the Pink Bead. It was Enolo with his companion, Latche. They both had beads that were shiny like the sun and other brown beads.

They were from south where the warm wind starts, and they had brown skin. Ollieoheh pulled the dead man's sleeve away from his skin to see what color he was, his skin was brown. Ollieoheh signed to Zugger, asking if they had bows and arrows. He nodded yes. They all stood there thinking…. *Would someone kill another person for his story beads?*

The river cut through a rocky outcropping exposing a vein of pink and black stone that went below the ground. For many winters the villagers chipped it out of the ground leaving big holes. Their settlement grew around those holes. The rocky area gave some protection from the wind and animals, but it wasn't very high. They had made a huge stone fence around their area with the extra rocks they didn't like. There were free standing buildings of stone, but most of them lived underground. They had a huge meat cache, they liked smoking meat and fish. Many people came to get the stone, some liked to dig it out. Men there were excellent flakers, their arrowheads were not only functional, they were beautiful. They made hide scrapers, knife blades and one man could make bolas. His name was Eegeegoo, his wife was Lieura. The bolas he made were rounded with a little knob on top for attaching sinew. They were so beautiful, people wanted them for amulets, he and his wife both wore one,

they were just too beautiful to throw at animals. Many people brought Eegeegoo special rocks from many places to flake. He found one rock that looked like a resting eagle.

He flaked the outside so it would sit up! His working area had three special window slots. He had thin bladders stretched tight and had rubbed them with fish oil to make them translucent for the sunlight to come in. He would use them until it was coldest of cold, the stone flaked easier in the cold. He would take them out completely when it was warm.

The night of the ringed moon, Tahecha said The Great Spirit was warning the people of a great change. *The next day the river ran away.* It left the fish lying dead, *everywhere.* However, as they walked on the empty riverbed, they saw it was *covered* with polished nodules of pink and black stones. *What would the settlement do with no water?*

All forty people in the Pink Bead settlement were in the empty river harvesting fish and picking up the beautiful polished rocks. They set up gutting tables right there and started cutting… The fish were not quite frozen, they were ready to smoke….. Some of the men went to an empty cave and got it ready for the biggest smoking area they ever had. They put rocks on the floor and then wood on them…they built quick log racks they could lay the fish on and went to another cave to start more. They cleaned another cave for storing the fish when they were finished. It was the very last cave. As quickly as they could they gathered up wood… their favorite was alder, but other woods would work. They had never tried to smoke fish this late in the winter, but there they were, ready!

They worked until it got too dark, they were all tired. In one day they had filled one cave with fish and started smoking them. The smell filled the air… they were thankful, very thankful… *the ring around the moon was a good omen.*

The next morning birds started coming from every direction. How could they know? A man stood at the gutting table with a tree limb swatting the birds that got too close. They took the guts in baskets down the river away from the settlement. The birds were big and aggressive. One grabbed the arm of the man with the basket, the talons dug deep into his flesh, and the bird tore at the man's face with his sharp beak. He fell to the ground, flailing at them… other birds flew to him and began pulling him apart…the man was screaming. More birds came, there were too many…the people ran back into the settlement for shelter, they had gotten enough fish….

To be continued…

About the Author

Clovis, New Mexico is where Cha was born. With great interest in crafts, she tanned hides, worked with buckskin and did hair. Cha learned to spin and weave in Mexico and taught weaving in Eastern New Mexico University. After living in New Mexico for twenty-eight years, she went to Alaska to learn to do gold work... Cha proved to be too creative and was let go from her position in the gold industry. She then had the opportunity to learn to carve. She loved fossil walrus ivory and bone from ancient animals. Most of the ivory was broken artifacts. She imagined that she was carving the faces of those ancient makers. She learned to "read" the artifacts and their stories. Later in life through DNA testing, she found her ancestors came from Siberia... Her Mother's geneology showed Cherokee blood....

CPSIA information can be obtained
at www.ICGtesting.com
Printed in the USA
272364LV00002B

9 781770 972261